# A Great Place To Work

## Improving Conditions for Staff in Young Children's Programs

*Revised Edition*

Paula Jorde Bloom

National Association for the Education of Young Children–Washington, D.C.

*Photo credits:* Robert Burgess 7; Paula Jorde Bloom 11, 32, 41, 43, 53, 51; Subjects & Predicates 18; Toni H. Liebman 28; Hildegard Adler 46; Renaud Thomas 58; Marja Bergen 63.



**National Association for the Education of Young Children**
**1509 16th Street, NW**
**Washington, DC 20036-1426**
**202-232-8777 or 800-424-2460**
**Website: www.naeyc.org**

Through its publications program the National Association for the Education of Young Children (NAEYC) provides a forum for discussion of major issues and ideas in the early childhood field, with the hope of provoking thought and promoting professional growth. The views expressed or implied are not necessarily those of the Association. NAEYC thanks the author, who donated much time and effort to develop this book as a contribution to the profession.

Library of Congress Catalog Number: 88-62481
ISBN 0-935989-18-8
NAEYC #250

Printed in the United States of America

# About the Author

**Paula Jorde Bloom** is a professor of early childhood education at National-Louis University in Wheeling, Illinois, where she teaches graduate courses in early childhood administration and serves as Director of the Center for Early Childhood Leadership. Dr. Bloom has taught preschool and kindergarten, designed and directed a child care center, and served as administrator of a campus laboratory school. She is the author of numerous journal articles and several widely read books including *Avoiding Burnout: Strategies for Managing Time, Space, and People* (New Horizons); *Blueprint for Action: Achieving Center-Based Change Through Staff Development* (with M. Sheerer and J. Britz) (New Horizons); and *Circle of Influence: Implementing Shared Decision Making and Participative Management* (New Horizons). Her most recent book, *Workshop Essentials,* provides tips and techniques for planning and presenting dynamic workshops.

# *Contents*

# *A NOTE FROM THE AUTHOR . . .*

*A Great Place to Work* was first published in 1988. Writing this updated, revised edition provided a good opportunity for me to reflect on the progress our field has made over the past decade on issues relating to the quality of work life for early childhood professionals. To be sure, high turnover, job stress, and low morale still plague our field, but there are many encouraging signs that things have changed in a positive direction.

Over the past few years, there has been a heightened awareness of the importance of the adult work environment as an indicator of early childhood program quality. This shift in thinking has been due in large part to the tenacious efforts of organizations like the Center for the Child Care Workforce, the National Association for the Education of Young Children, and the Center for Career Development in Early Care and Education. Child advocates have made important strides in informing and educating parents, program administrators, policymakers, and the public at large about the link between caregivers' needs and children's needs.

Recent developments in the field provide strong evidence that the message is being heard. In several states, for example, legislative initiatives have been launched to increase early childhood teachers' compensation and benefits. Across the country, quality enhancement grants from the philanthropic community have been targeted to improving conditions for early childhood staff. The corporate community, as well, has made a notable financial investment in funding initiatives to stem turnover and improve the professional competence of teaching and administrative staff in early childhood programs.

These are very promising developments, but there is still much to be done before the message in this book becomes obsolete. In this revised edition, I have made several changes to reflect the current state of the field. I have updated references and resources and added a new chapter summarizing recent research on the differing perceptions of directors and teachers.

While the primary audience for this book is the director of a center-based program, I am aware that this slim volume has been quite popular as a supplemental college text. Indeed, a discussion of informal and formal work climate assessments can serve as an excellent discussion starter for classes and workshops in early childhood program administration. Even without the benefit of a particular center to evaluate, students can become better acquainted with the components essential to establishing and maintaining a professional environment in any work setting and, by reflecting on the value of each dimension, shape their professional managerial styles. Self-awareness and professional growth are logical extensions of this important work.

I deeply appreciate all the wonderful ideas and helpful suggestions I have received from center directors around the country since *A Great Place to Work* was first published. Their hard work to improve the quality of work life at their centers has been the impetus for my research and writing. Their insights have enriched my own professional development; their real-life scenarios continue to keep me grounded in reality. For that I am indebted.

*—Paula Jorde Bloom*
*January 1997*

# *For Program Directors . . .*

As an educator, you are well aware that the quality of your program has a tremendous effect on what young children learn and how they develop. Fortunately, many excellent resources are available to help you evaluate and improve the quality of the learning environment you provide for young children (Bredekamp & Copple 1997; NAEYC 1998).

As part of a constant process to upgrade your program, you must also view your efforts from another perspective—the quality of the professional environment in which you and your staff work. Because the human factor is the most critical factor in quality child care, programs that are sensitive to the needs of adults are in a far better position to provide optimal learning environments for children.

You know that early childhood education is a demanding profession, physically and emotionally. Therefore, the personal and professional growth of those charged with educating young children needs constant attention. All of us must demonstrate every day how we value the work that our colleagues do with young children and their families. In the words of the National Child Care Staffing Study, "By failing to meet the needs of the adults who work in child care, we are threatening not only their well-being, but that of the children in their care" (Whitebook, Howes, & Phillips 1989, 3).

If you have been directing an early childhood program for even a short time, you are well aware that the national picture of early childhood work environments is bleak. Staff turnover continues to plague the field. Many programs experience a constant strain as they search for and train new staff. Continuity of care for children, a critical variable in quality, is clearly jeopardized in programs that experience high turnover.

The strenuous work, low pay, lack of benefits, and difficult working conditions all take their toll. When staff feel overwhelmed, tense, and tired, their commitment to the profession soon wanes. Low morale, stress, and even job burnout can result.

It is ironic that teachers often experience a feeling of professional accomplishment from their interactions with children but still feel a profound sense of personal failure because the conditions of teaching are so often frustrating, unrewarding, and intolerably difficult. It is their inability to fulfill their aspirations that drives many talented teachers from the profession and fosters a kind of cynicism in those who remain.

Indeed, unless we better understand how the quality of work life affects us and how we supervise and teach, our very survival as a profession may be at stake. Because you are in a leadership role at your center, the responsibility for reversing this trend rests squarely on your shoulders. Of course, this makes your demanding job even more complicated. Untangling the web of relationships between work and worker is no easy task.

This book is intended to help you sort out the important issues, to evaluate your work environment from the perspective of your employees, and to improve it for the benefit of staff, parents, and children.

Our discussion has four parts. Chapter 1 provides an overview of the concept of organizational climate and the way this theoretical construct can serve as a framework for both describing and evaluating early childhood work settings. Ten dimensions of climate are described, with examples drawn from a variety of early childhood settings.

Chapter 2 stresses the importance of regularly assessing work attitudes and how climate assessment can be used as a yardstick with which to measure organizational improvement. You can assess the organizational climate of your center by using either the informal or formal survey provided in this book or by designing your own. Guidelines for the assessment process stress the need for confidentiality and the importance of the staff's active participation in interpreting the survey results.

One of the more interesting patterns to emerge in the research conducted on organizational climate over the past decade is the difference in perceptions that administrators and teachers have of different organizational practices. Chapter 3 summarizes this research and discusses some of the reasons why individuals in different positions may view the world so differently.

The final chapter provides guidelines for creating and maintaining a healthy work climate. This chapter includes a wealth of ideas that will help you and your staff implement change in healthy and constructive ways. By addressing the personal and professional needs of all involved, teachers and administrators can work collaboratively to create their own Great Place to Work.

# 1

# What It Takes to Create and Maintain a Healthy Work Climate

## WHAT IS ORGANIZATIONAL CLIMATE?

If you have visited many other early childhood programs, you know that each has its own personality. Some seem to exude excitement and energy from the moment you walk in the door. The director and teachers are spirited, vital, and energetic. Staff are dynamic, happy, and enthusiastic about their work. When they talk with children, parents, and each other, they are warm and supportive.

In other settings, discontent and tension seem to permeate the air. The mood appears to be competitive and harsh. Staff and parents mistrust and resent each other. Complaints about staff roles, responsibilities, and general work conditions are frequent.

Each program's personality and characteristics certainly affect the quality of work life for the staff. Organizational theorists refer to the distinct atmosphere that characterizes work settings as *organizational climate* (Tagiuri 1978; Anderson 1982; Joyce & Slocum 1984; Hoy, Tarter, & Kottkamp 1991). The use of a weather metaphor seems appropriate, because some centers are distinctly sunny, warm, and nurturing while others are stormy and unpredictable.

Most of us do not stop to analyze the organizational climate in which we work, but the climate does influence our behavior: our feelings about work; how comfortable we feel in expressing our opinions; our relationships with children, parents, and co-workers; and how well we perform our responsibilities.

Although organizational climate may be relatively easy to notice even in a brief visit, the concept is not easy to define. It is made up of many dimensions, including the perceptions, attitudes, beliefs, and values of all individuals within a given work setting—a composite of personalities and the leadership that guides them.

Some theorists define organizational climate as a *global perception* of the perceived quality of an organization (James & Jones 1974; Tagiuri 1978). This does not mean, however, that climate is unidimensional. Many different organizational practices contribute to the global perception people have of their work environment.

It is important to remember that these perceptions are *subjective interpretations* that may vary between people and with reality. Individuals perceive the meaning of events differently, depending on their role in the organization, their value orientation, and the context of the situation. It has been found, for example, that directors consistently view organizational practices more favorably than do teachers. This research is described in greater detail in Chapter 3.

Organizational climate is not the same as psychological climate or job satisfaction (Jones & James 1979; Schneider & Reichers 1983; Pope & Stremmel 1992), which are individual perceptions of the degree to which individual needs and expectations are met. Organizational climate, on the other hand, describes conditions that exist in the workplace based on the *collective perceptions* of workers.

Organizational climate and job satisfaction, however, are closely related. Although it is not clear whether climate or satisfaction comes first, job satisfaction seems to be higher in schools with relatively open climates. These climates are characterized by a sense of belonging, many opportunities to interact, autonomy, and upward influence (Coughlan & Cooke 1974; Hoy, Tarter, & Kottkamp 1991).

Whenever people work together, they individually and jointly affect each other and their environment. Job descriptions may define different jobs, but individuals shape their roles according to their skills and attitudes. Each person influences the collective values and work orientation of the group. At the same time, people's attitudes and behavior are shaped by the environments in which they work.

This pattern of relationships has been called a social-ecological model of human behavior because it stresses the dynamic, interactive nature between people and their environment (Lewin 1951; Bronfenbrenner 1981; Moos 1986). The model fits well with the concept of organizational climate because the collective perceptions of workers are influenced by differences in organizational structure as well as by individual meanings that people attach to their interactions.

## DIMENSIONS OF ORGANIZATIONAL CLIMATE

To better understand the dimensions of organizational climate, we must take into account the research and theoretical work on school effectiveness, group dynamics, work attitudes, and the interplay between people and their environments (Fox 1974; Tagiuri 1978; Anderson 1982; Moos 1986).

The 10 dimensions described in Table 1 on page 4 arise from a practical sense of how early childhood centers differ from and are consistent with present theoretical knowledge about individual and group behavior in organizations. There is certainly some overlap between these 10 dimensions, as they are not meant to be mutually exclusive categories.

### Collegiality

People are social. All of us need to feel that others care about us and are concerned about our welfare. Emotional support, therefore, is a potent force in creating a positive work climate. When staff support and trust one another, an esprit de corps develops. The rationale for providing an environment that fosters friendly, supportive relationships is well grounded in research about job satisfaction and self-fulfillment (Little 1982; Rosenholtz 1989).

In addition, compelling research evidence indicates that collegiality is characteristic of effective, high-achieving elementary schools

## *Table 1.*
## The Ten Dimensions of Organizational Climate

| *Dimension* | *Definition* | *Related Research* |
|---|---|---|
| **Collegiality** | The extent to which staff are friendly, are supportive, and trust one another. The peer cohesion and esprit de corps of the group. | Little (1982); Goodlad (1983); Zahorick (1984); Rosenholtz (1989) |
| **Professional Growth Opportunities** | The degree of emphasis placed on personal and professional growth. The extent to which opportunities are available to increase professional competence. | Kent (1985); Arnett (1989); Rosenholtz (1989); Joyce (1990); Fullan (1991); Morgan et al. (1993) |
| **Supervisor Support** | The degree of facilitative leadership that provides encouragement, support, and clear expectations. | Zigarmi (1981); Fleischer (1985); Kozlowski & Doherty (1989); Sheerer & Bloom (1997) |
| **Clarity** | The extent to which policies, procedures, and responsibilities are clearly defined and communicated. | Pettegrew & Wolf (1982); Schwab & Iwanicki (1982); Stremmel, Benson, & Powell (1993) |
| **Reward System** | The degree of fairness and equity in the distribution of pay, fringe benefits, and opportunities for advancement. | Modigliani (1986); Stern (1986); Huseman & Hatfield (1989); Whitebook, Howes, & Phillips (1989); Bloom (1993a,b) |
| **Decisionmaking** | The degree of autonomy given to staff and the extent to which they are involved in making centerwide decisions. | Neugebauer (1975); Rosenholtz (1989); Conley (1991); Smylie (1992); Ferrara & Repa (1993); Bloom (1995) |
| **Goal Consensus** | The degree to which staff agree on the philosophy, goals, and objectives of the center. | Neugebauer (1975); Silver & Moyle (1984); Rosenholtz (1989) |
| **Task Orientation** | The emphasis placed on good planning, efficiency, and getting the job done. | Nash (1983); Moos (1986); Lee, Buck, & Midgley (1992); Wien (1995) |
| **Physical Setting** | The extent to which the spatial arrangement of the center helps or hinders staff in carrying out their responsibilities. | Steele (1973); Weinstein (1979); Phyfe-Perkins (1980); Prescott (1981) |
| **Innovativeness** | The extent to which the center adapts to change and encourages staff to find creative ways to solve problems. | Berman & McLaughlin (1978); Young & Kasten (1980); Jorde (1984); Fullan (1991); Rogers (1995) |

(Little 1982; Goodlad 1983). For example, in effective schools, teachers value and participate in a great range of professional interactions with one another—they plan together, talk about instruction, and engage in structured observations of one another.

Schools with a strong sense of collegiality are characterized by a unified team spirit, a collective sense of efficacy, and the absence of social cliques. Interactions are comfortable and individuals feel free to express their thoughts openly. These schools give high priority to minimizing teacher isolation.

These same patterns of collegiality undoubtedly characterize effective early childhood programs. Within all these settings, the appropriate degree of collegiality varies depending on the formal and informal structures of the program and the needs and expectations of the staff.

## Opportunities for professional growth

In some schools for young children, teachers are unaware of what other teachers are doing in the classroom, and they rarely share ideas and resources. In contrast, centers that value professional development find creative ways to pay staff expenses for conferences and workshops, to provide release time to visit other programs, to reimburse tuition for college courses, and to stock a library with a variety of professional magazines, journals, and curriculum guides.

Research has shown that the degree of emphasis on opportunities for professional growth appears most closely related to management priorities (Little 1982; Griffin 1983; Fullan 1991). Schools that have a strong professional orientation give high priority to maximizing opportunities for teachers to reflect on and evaluate their own instructional practices. These programs plan opportunities for staff to expand their knowledge base and widen their repertoire of competencies. At the same time, they create a nonthreatening atmosphere in which staff are encouraged to help one another.

High-growth climates also gear inservice staff-development activities to individual experience and tie opportunities for professional advancement to a well-defined career ladder. These climates encourage staff to stretch and develop their potential.

Although staff development is usually advocated as a way to improve teachers' skill in working with children, it also should be recognized as an important ingredient in a satisfying and stimulating professional life. Staff development that is designed to solve practical problems and to meet the personal needs of teachers can make an important contribution both to the quality of teaching in schools and to the satisfaction that teachers feel with their professional lives.

## Supervisor support

One of the most important ingredients supporting high-quality early childhood programming is facilitative leadership that provides clear expectations, support, and encouragement of staff. All of us need to know we are valued for our hard work, but we need more than mere recognition. A supportive supervisor gives open, honest, and regular feedback that is respectful of the individual's self-worth and provides direction for personal and professional change.

Increasing the quality and quantity of feedback to teachers achieves several goals. It not only provides teachers with needed recognition but broadens their repertoire of instructional strategies that can improve effectiveness. Moreover, it sends a clear message that their work is valued.

Many early childhood programs are so tightly staffed that new teachers and assistants are turned loose in the classroom with little orientation or ongoing coherent supervision and training. This often happens even though we know that frequent, useful, and fair evaluations are essential to guide teaching behavior and improve effectiveness with children.

In fact, lack of supervisor support for training, career guidance, and interpreting policies has been found to be a major cause of job turnover in the field (Fleischer 1985). Teachers who leave may have a lower sense of accomplishment because they did not receive clear performance feedback.

Teacher attitudes toward their supervisors can have a positive effect on their performance and job satisfaction. Indeed, a supervisor's psychological support may well have a more enduring impact on a teacher's self-esteem and overall performance than any tangible resources provided (Coughlan & Cooke 1974).

***Good staff development contributes to the quality of teaching and increases professional satisfaction.***

The quality of the supervisor–teacher relationship has consistently been found to be strongly related to teachers' level of job satisfaction and their teaching performance at all levels of the educational spectrum. For example, in effective elementary schools, principals devote more time to observing teachers, discuss more work problems with teachers, are more supportive of teachers' efforts to improve, and are more active in setting up evaluation procedures than are principals in less effective schools (Purkey & Smith 1982; Silver & Moyle 1984; Fullan 1991). It is also important for teachers to have supervisors they regard not only as supportive but also as competent.

The implications of this research for facilitative leadership in early childhood programs are clear. Preschool programs with supervisor support are organized for steady improvement; they build and nurture professional competence through clear, direct, and unambiguous feedback that focuses on behavior and action. Directors in these centers act as instructional leaders to guide staff performance.

## Clarity

Every early childhood program operates with a complex network of roles and relationships, so the way policies, procedures, and responsibilities are defined and carried out deeply affects the program's effectiveness. Only when roles and responsibilities are clearly defined can employees understand how the nature and scope of their individual jobs mesh with the expectations of others.

Lack of clear job descriptions can create conflict among staff. If policies or procedures are vague, problems arise when people try to communicate. Poorly defined rules and regulations can result in confusion and add to job stress. In contrast, order and clarity are positively related to job satisfaction and performance (Schwab & Iwanicki 1982; Moos 1986). Thus, effective management practices in this area can have a direct impact on reducing role-related stress.

Why is clarity so important in early childhood education? In most programs, assistants, teachers, and lead teachers may all have similar duties ranging from maintenance work to planning curriculum and conducting parent conferences. Tension often results when title and pay do not distinguish between who does what, why, and when. In our field, distinctions in responsibilities based on job title are related more to the quantity of time spent performing tasks than to the nature of the tasks themselves (Whitebook et al. 1982).

The National Child Care Staffing Study (Whitebook, Howes, & Phillips 1989) found that 70% of the teaching staff included in the sample worked without a written contract, and 40% had no written job description. Stremmel, Benson, and Powell (1993) found that the frequency of communication at a center (for example, the number of staff meetings held) was related to employees' positive work attitudes.

Communication in programs with a strong organizational climate is consistent, clear, and unambiguous. There is agreement among staff about who is to do what, how, and when. Information is direct and open and flows both vertically (upward and downward) and horizontally (among employees in similar positions).

Of course, clarity is not something that can be achieved and then forgotten. Roles, responsibilities, and regulations must constantly be updated to meet the changing needs of a healthy workplace.

## Reward system

Early childhood educators stay in the profession for reasons other than salaries, fringe benefits, tenure and job security, promotion opportunities, and prestige, but they often leave for such reasons. A number of studies have consistently found that most early childhood workers feel underpaid and undervalued by society (Kontos & Stremmel 1988; Whitebook, Howes, & Phillips 1989; Cost, Quality, & Child Outcomes Team 1995).

Professional and advocacy organizations such as the National Association for the Education of Young Children (NAEYC) and the Center for the Child Care Workforce (CCW) consider salaries and working conditions priority issues. Our society obviously must resolve some deep and complicated problems about the funding of early childhood programs and the status of child care workers. Both prospective and practicing teachers are influenced by salary levels. The number of teachers who leave for other occupations is directly related to salary, as is the number of new entrants into the profession.

Even as we wrestle with these issues on a national basis, center directors and policymaking boards can take steps to assure their staff fair and just employment and salary policies. Healthy organizational climates include a reward system with fair and equitably administered pay, job security, and promotion policies.

Although the importance of pay as a source of motivation is often downplayed in teacher self-reports of job satisfaction, the extrinsic rewards workers receive are important for their symbolic value. Pay symbolizes esteem—the value society places on teaching.

Money means different things to different people. For some it is a powerful motivator that can buy status and security. For others it is a legitimate form of recognition. Money also has symbolic value because it is an important indicator of equity.

Teachers compare wages, both within and outside the program. For many workers, questions of equity may be just as important as questions of adequacy (Huseman & Hatfield 1989). Some workers may even unconsciously or consciously match their efforts to their perceptions about their pay.

Opportunities for promotion can also have strong symbolic importance. Many teachers regard promotion as recognition of past performance. For others, opportunities for advancement offer a sense of future security. For some teachers, especially those in the early stages of their careers, the likelihood of promotion may be more important than current wages.

## Decisionmaking

Who makes what kind of decisions? The decisionmaking structure of an early childhood program determines how power is distributed and how much influence the teaching and administrative staff have in making decisions that impact program functioning. Decisions may have to do with staff supervision and professional development; instructional practices, grouping, and scheduling; fiscal policies and practices; human resource allocation; centerwide goals and educational objectives; school–home and school–community relations; facilities management; and evaluation practices regarding individual children, the staff, or the center as a whole (Bloom 1995).

In general, when teachers feel that their program's decisionmaking structure is fair and encourages staff input, they are likely to share a commitment to implement program goals. Centers with positive organizational climates encourage staff to take an active role in centerwide decisionmaking. Research suggests that this will also have a positive impact on the level of job satisfaction staff experience (Whitebook et al. 1982; Whitebook, Howes, & Phillips 1989).

As we will see in Chapter 3, some discrepancies are typical in this area. Administrators and staff may not agree on how decisionmaking influence is distributed; and, from the employees' perspective, the actual and desired amount of influence may differ. Most workers desire more involvement in decisionmaking, especially regarding issues that directly affect them.

In positive work environments, the decisionmaking structure is flexible rather than rigid. It responds to workers' concerns and issues and takes into consideration the changing expertise, abilities, needs, and expectations of all concerned.

***When teachers feel that their program's decisionmaking structure is fair and encourages staff input, they are likely to share a commitment to implement program goals and be more satisfied with their jobs.***

## Goal consensus

The degree to which staff, administrators, and the board agree on the goals of the center is closely related to the decisionmaking dimension of organizational climate. The flip side of goal consensus is conflict and divisiveness.

All employees need to hold a common vision for the program so their efforts can be consistently directed toward goals. Educational goals establish priorities—what we want children to do, to be, or to have as a result of their early childhood experience.

Differences in philosophy, socioeconomic status, background, and tradition are bound to contribute to differences in value orientation. Goal consensus thus reflects the ability of a staff to compromise and tolerate differences of opinion so that individuals can work toward a common vision.

Previous research provides clues as to how goal consensus may impact the quality of teaching practices and overall program effectiveness in educational settings. In elementary schools, Rosenholtz (1989) has found that ambiguous goals and a lack of unifying purpose lead to greater instructional uncertainty. In such schools, teachers tend to define and independently pursue their own goals. This reinforces norms of self-reliance rather than collaboration. The result is reduced professional interaction and feelings of isolation.

## Task orientation

Good planning, efficiency, and getting the job done are the essence of task orientation. In early childhood programs with a positive organizational climate, time is used wisely and staff are not burdened with unnecessary busywork. Meetings are well planned and purposeful, and procrastination is an exception rather than the rule.

On the other hand, it is also possible for work environments to be obsessed with efficiency. These workplaces are too rigid and controlling and create a stifling work atmosphere. When this kind of "punch-clock" mentality exists, staff are expected to adhere to strict schedules, and time is viewed as a scarce resource. Such an atmosphere can foreclose opportunities for spontaneous activity and reduce the empowerment of staff (Wien 1995).

A positive work climate balances efficiency and clear organization with flexibility. Just as teachers and parents expect children to work up to their potential, staff perform at their best when the program operates efficiently, personnel are used effectively, and activities are coordinated so that people are neither overloaded nor idle. In a healthy organization, everyone works hard, but there is a good fit between people's own dispositions and the demands of the program.

## Physical setting

Spatial arrangement can play a powerful role in shaping attitudes about work and influencing moods, dispositions, and employee morale. Although research in business and industry shows that favorable attitudes toward buildings, facilities, materials, and equipment seldom produce the type of job satisfaction that improve work performance, this may not be the case in early childhood education.

Why? Because the spatial arrangement in a program strongly influences children's behavior and therefore the teacher's ability to carry out program objectives. Temperature, light, color, noise, ventilation, design, and furniture layout can help or hinder staff and children as they work. Poorly equipped environments, or those that have insufficient or ineffectively used space, are frustrating and stressful places to work.

Early childhood programs that have a positive organizational climate on the physical setting dimension pay particular attention to the importance of the spatial arrangement and design of the classroom and support space. Areas are orderly, well organized, and furnished with the proper equipment, materials, and resources for staff to do their work effectively.

Physical setting can also reflect the overall climate of an organization. When people work in a place that they perceive to be negative and unsatisfying, they tend not to want to take care of their environment. The building may appear run down, drab, or "institutional." Thus, physical appearance may well be a good indicator of the general organizational health of the program.

## Innovativeness

Early childhood centers, like all organizations, must adapt to change in order to survive. An innovative atmosphere encourages people to find creative ways to solve problems. Diversity is valued, so new educational approaches and techniques are welcomed. In contrast, poor climates are often characterized by complacency, conformity, and a rigid adherence to tradition. In subtle ways, they discourage people from offering ideas and providing suggestions on ways to improve program practices.

Administrators can initiate or inhibit change. They can build or erode a sense of innovativeness in their staff, and they can encourage or stifle experimentation. Research conducted at the elementary and secondary levels has found that the degree of a program's innovativeness primarily depends on a leadership style that encourages receptivity to new ideas rather than on the size or level of the school's financial resources (Berman & McLaughlin 1978; Fullan 1991).

In examining differences between effective and less effective high schools, for example, Lightfoot (1983) found that what distinguished exemplary schools was their "consciousness of imperfection"—their willingness to look at their imperfections and create a climate of continual improvement.

Research at the early childhood level, as well, reveals that the degree of innovativeness of a program is directly linked to the leadership style of its director (Jorde 1984). Directors are typically the ones who sense the need for change, set the pace for the change process, and then monitor progress as each new idea is translated into action (Schrag, Nelson, & Siminowsky 1985). Innovative directors are responsive to the concerns of teachers, parents, and the community. They empower people to analyze problems and plan corrective action.

## ORGANIZATIONAL CLIMATE AND ACCREDITATION STATUS

There is ample anecdotal evidence that the accreditation self-study process promotes positive changes in programs, and those changes have been linked to beneficial outcomes for both children and staff (Carter 1986; Bundy 1988; Herr, Johnson, & Zimmerman 1993). When data from a U.S. General Accounting Office study of 208 accredited centers is compared to other national samples, it ap-

## *Figure 1.*

## A Comparison of Organizational Climate by Accreditation Status*

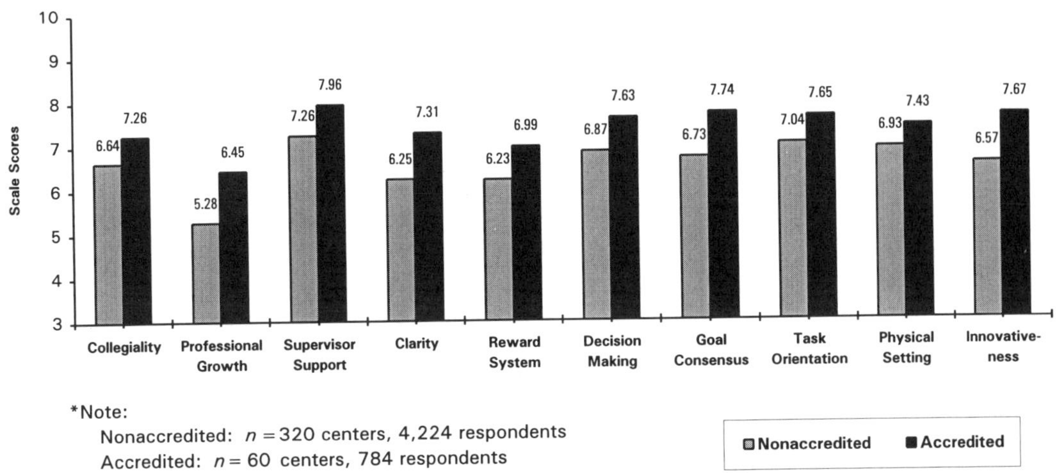


pears that accredited programs not only pay their teachers more but they also provide a more comprehensive benefits package (Willer et al. 1991; Powell et al. 1994). Accredited centers tend to have better trained staff, pay higher wages, have lower staff turnover, and provide higher quality caregiving for children than do nonaccredited centers (Whitebook, Phillips, & Howes 1993).

Research looking specifically at accreditation status as it relates to the organizational climate dimensions described in this chapter has also found strong differences between programs (Bloom 1996b). A study of 60 accredited and 320 nonaccredited child care centers revealed notable differences between accredited and nonaccredited programs relating to the quality of work life for staff.

Figure 1 shows that in all 10 dimensions of organizational climate, the staff at accredited programs expressed more positive perceptions of their work life. The four dimensions that together accounted for the greatest variation in differences were innovativeness, goal consensus, opportunities for professional growth, and clarity.

Strong differences were also registered in the level of job commitment and staff turnover between accredited and nonaccredited programs.

Taken together with the anecdotal evidence on accreditation, it appears that the accreditation process transforms programs from the inside out, making staff active partners in the program improvement activities. While improved program quality for children is the primary goal of accreditation, an improved quality of work life for staff seems to be an ancillary benefit.

* * *

The 10 dimensions of organizational climate are critical in every professional early childhood work environment. Each clearly affects the staff's morale and their ability to effectively teach young children.

Now that we have looked at some of the factors that determine whether work environments are personally and professionally satisfying, we can begin to assess how well our own programs measure up in these dimensions.

# 2

# HOW TO MEASURE THE ORGANIZATIONAL CLIMATE OF YOUR PROGRAM

## ASSESSING WORK ATTITUDES

A great deal of work has been done to evaluate organizational climate in both business and industry (Bowditch & Buono 1982; Nash 1983; Seashore et al. 1983). Other assessment instruments have been developed that focus on the organizational climate of elementary and secondary schools (Moos 1979; Fraser, Anderson, & Walberg 1982; Gottfredson 1984; Wilson, Firestone, & Herriott 1984; Howard, Howell, & Brainard 1987; Hoy, Tarter, & Kottkamp 1991).

Until recently, however, little attention has been given to the unique aspects of early childhood work settings as they relate to overall organizational climate. Early childhood programs are strikingly different from other environments in areas such as funding structure, decisionmaking hierarchy, supervision methods, professional roles, and the nature of the work. Therefore, most of the instruments listed above are not practical for assessing the quality of our unique professional work climate.

This chapter provides an overview of the importance of assessing work attitudes. We will look at the benefits of both

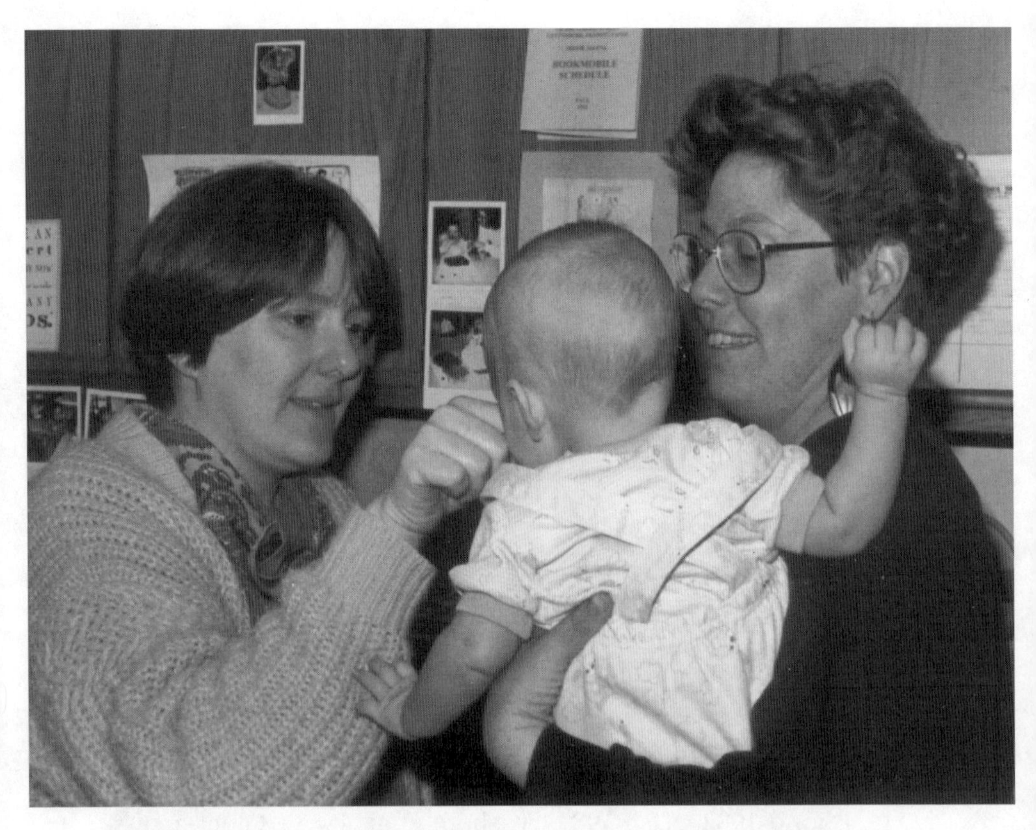

***Staying in close contact with parents helps the administrator to know what is going well and what needs to be improved.***

informal and formal assessments and will describe one assessment tool—intended to be used specifically in schools and centers for young children—as an example of the process.

The ideas in this chapter are valuable for directors as they make decisions about the daily operation of their programs for young children. The informal and formal surveys described in this chapter bring to life the ways in which the 10 dimensions of organizational climate outlined in Chapter 1 can be used to evaluate program effectiveness. The implications for implementing these dimensions are discussed in greater detail in Chapter 4.

## The benefits of assessing work attitudes

Every good early childhood program administrator wants to know where things are going well and where there may be need for improvement. As director, you probably have an overall impression that things are going well or not so well, but you may lack specific information on just what areas of the program contribute to those impressions. The information gleaned from assessing work attitudes can help you clarify those vague feelings and define more precisely how different dimensions of your center are perceived.

Staff members' perceptions of a program's work climate are a good source of information not because they reflect objective reality but rather because what people perceive as their experience is what is important. A systematic method to measure staff perceptions of organizational climate can be extremely useful to

- clarify feelings about work,
- gauge personal and organizational efficiency and effectiveness,
- help explain why and where things are going well,
- identify where changes are needed,
- promote better problem solving,
- increase staff involvement,
- give direction about program priorities,
- target areas for staff development,
- improve overall morale and staff performance, and
- help ensure that the center stays healthy.

To solve problems and handle conflicts more effectively, directors must establish a climate that invites feedback and supports an open discussion of differences. When issues are not dealt with openly, teachers can feel manipulated. Such feelings can diminish their commitment to the center.

One valuable insight gained during an assessment of employee attitudes about their work environment is a sharper understanding of where perceptions differ between administrators and employees. One of the more common findings, for example, is that directors often believe they give far more feedback to their staff than the teachers perceive they get. Another common difference is found in directors' and staff's perceptions regarding staff involvement in decisions about different organizational policies and practices. In Chapter 3 we will see that directors typically rate the organizational climate of their programs more favorably than do their teachers.

The objectives, content, and emphasis of inservice programs for staff development can all be shaped by analyzing the work climate. The assessment process also helps directors and staff answer important questions that will aid them in establishing center priorities. Which issues are most pressing? How can the center's resources be used to best advantage? Where is additional support needed?

Even if you are not aware of any immediate problems, periodic surveys of work attitudes are helpful. One way to ensure that your center stays healthy is to regularly monitor employee perceptions of organizational practices. When used in this way, the assessment can be preventive by directing energies away from griping and toward finding solutions before issues develop into problems. Two-way communication between director and staff can increase simply because all are engaged in the common task of improving their own work environment.

## COMPONENTS OF A GOOD SURVEY

To produce beneficial results, an attitude survey must meet three requirements.

***Surveys must have a clear purpose.*** The purpose of the procedure should be stated clearly and understood by all concerned, including boards of directors or others involved in the operation of the program. The process should convey to employees that feedback is important to improve the efficiency and effectiveness of the center. It should be clearly stated that the results will not be used to embarrass people or to undermine individuals who have problems. Surveys should be intended for constructive purposes, to prevent apprehension and defensiveness and ensure wholehearted participation.

***Responses must be confidential.*** Accurate information can be obtained only when respondents are certain that their answers will be anonymous. Therefore, any questionnaire should be scored by a disinterested person who will maintain complete confidence about the results. Otherwise, the information will be distorted and of limited value.

***Information about results must be shared.*** Results (favorable or unfavorable) must be shared with the entire group. By doing so, an administrator indicates concern for staff welfare and conveys the intent to be open and to support needed changes. This step can in itself contribute to healthier staff relations by opening channels of communication and stimulating group problem solving.

When the results are translated into follow-up activities, teachers feel a greater sense of professional investment and shared responsibility to implement change and incorporate new practices.

## PLANNING FOR THE ASSESSMENT

Directors have used a variety of approaches to collect information about how staff perceive their professional work climate. You will probably want to do this at least once a year, preferably at the same time each year.

One way to initiate the process is to describe the assessment activity at a staff meeting or in a memo to each staff member. Either way, briefly comment on why organizational assessment can benefit everyone, how confidentiality will be maintained, what will happen with the information collected, and why it is important for everyone to participate. Staff also need to be told about the logistics of when and where to complete the survey. A sample letter is included in Appendix A.

You may want to distribute the survey at a staff meeting. If you do, make sure that everyone has enough time to fill it out and sufficient privacy to keep her or his responses confidential. Each person should receive a plain envelope in which to return the questionnaire to you or a staff representative.

If you give out a survey at the end of the day, ask that staff members not discuss their responses with each other and that all surveys be returned to you or the staff representative in a plain envelope the next day. Unless at least 80% of the staff return their surveys, the results will not be very helpful to you.

No matter how you administer your climate survey, it is best to have a disinterested party score it to be certain that confidentiality is maintained. Staff must feel free to answer the questions honestly, or the results may be inaccurate. An impartial outsider, such as a local college instructor or respected professional colleague, should score the responses.

## CONDUCTING AN INFORMAL SURVEY

Designing your own survey allows you to tailor questions to address specific elements of your program and even to target types of jobs—assistants, teachers, support staff, and administrators; or staff who work with various age groups; or full-time, part-time, and volunteer workers.

Directors who conduct informal assessments typically want to incorporate staff ideas when they design their questionnaires. Together you can select key questions about your program that tap into each of the dimensions discussed in Chapter 1 and listed in Table 1.

Items can be worded either in a forced-response format (yes/no, multiple choice, or ranking on a scale) or as open-ended questions. Forced-response questions are easier to score and help ensure consistency in interpretation, but sometimes none of the answers quite describe the individual's opinion. Open-ended questions are difficult to score and make it more likely that the individual can be identified but may elicit more specific comments.

An example of an informal assessment instrument is included in Appendix B. Feel free to reproduce copies of it to use with your staff. It is important to remember, however, that this short, informal survey provides only a global assessment of organizational climate. It should not be used to interpret organizational functioning in each of the 10 dimensions separately.

Periodically, you may decide that you want a more systematic, standardized assessment of your center's work climate that provides a more comprehensive analysis of organizational functioning. If so, the Early Childhood Work Environment Survey (ECWES) may suit your needs.

## USING THE EARLY CHILDHOOD WORK ENVIRONMENT SURVEY

The Early Childhood Work Environment Survey evolved from research conducted by the Early Childhood Professional Development Project (ECPDP) at National-Louis University. Its development was shaped by the need for an assessment instrument that could both describe and differentiate settings along several dimensions, demonstrate a satisfactory level of statistical reliability and validity, and serve as a useful tool for the profession to monitor and improve work settings.

Items on the survey were drawn from interview data collected during early exploratory research and from several other organizational climate scales. The research of Halpin and Croft (1963); Moos (1979, 1986); Seashore, Lawler, Mirvis, and Cammann (1983); and Wilson, Firestone, and Herriott (1984) was particularly valuable. Information about the field tests, norm-referencing procedures, and recent research establishing the validity of this survey is available elsewhere (Pope & Stremmel 1992; Dunn 1995; Bloom 1996a, 1996b).

The ECWES is copyrighted and thus may not be reproduced to distribute to your staff. Copies of it should be obtained from, and scored by, the Early Childhood Professional Development Project. The ECPDP will tabulate results in about six weeks. A nominal fee is charged for this computerized service. All records and results remain confidential. For further information, contact the Early Childhood Professional Development Project of National-Louis University at 1000 Capitol Drive, Wheeling, Illinois 60090.

### Administering and scoring the ECWES

The ECWES is designed for all administrators, teachers, and support staff (secretary, cook, maintenance staff) paid to work more than 10 hours a week in a program for young children. Centers with fewer than seven employees will probably find the survey less helpful because the results generally vary only slightly.

This survey is completed by each individual in private and takes approximately 15 minutes to fill out. Appendix C contains a sample copy of the survey, including a letter for administrators. Appendix D is a sample of the Work Environment Profile summarizing the data that a center would receive.

## The Work Environment Profile

Because the Early Childhood Work Environment Survey analyzes the professional environment of a center, the responses of individuals are compiled into one center profile that reflects group perceptions of current organizational practices. As you will note in Appendix D, the profile includes information on how workers perceive their work environment, how this setting compares to what they consider to be ideal, and how their center compares with other centers that have completed the survey.

Let us now turn to a closer look at each part of the Work Environment Profile. Even if you have designed your own instrument or are using another one, you will find this discussion helpful in interpreting your results.

***Part A. Organizational Climate.*** This portion of the profile includes a summary of the results to questions pertaining to the 10 dimensions of organizational climate. It describes the current organizational climate as measured by staff perceptions along each dimension. To make dimension scores comparable, all scores have been standardized on a common metric. The vertical axis indicates that the lowest possible score for each dimension is 0 and the highest possible score is 10. The vertical line for each dimension indicates the range of scores (low and high) for the participating center. The circle represents the mean score on this dimension for 5,251 early childhood workers who have completed the ECWES. The *X* shows the average rating of the respondents from the participating center with respect to each dimension.

The number of respondents' surveys used for Part A on the Work Environment Profile is indicated by the notation *N* = . If this number differs from the total number of staff who completed surveys, it may be because some surveys were incomplete or filled out incorrectly.

Incomplete surveys are not used in the data analysis for each section. The following provides a fuller explanation of how to interpret the ratings for each dimension.

*Collegiality.* This dimension measures the extent to which staff are friendly, supportive, and trusting of one another. A high score indicates that staff feel free to express their feelings and that they believe communication is generally frank and candid. Individuals working at centers with a high rating on the collegiality dimension usually feel that morale is high and that a strong sense of team spirit characterizes work relationships.

*Professional growth.* This category measures the extent to which professional growth opportunities are available to the staff. Centers that score high on this dimension provide regular staff-development workshops, encourage staff to share resources with one another, provide release time for teachers to attend conferences and visit other schools, and provide financial support and guidance for professional advancement.

*Supervisor support.* The collective perception of workers at centers scoring high on this dimension is that the supervision they receive is both supportive and helpful. Individuals who rank supervisor support positively feel that high but reasonable standards are set and that staff are helped to develop their skills. A low rating on this dimension may indicate that the supervisor does not provide enough feedback or that he or she is too critical and hard to please.

*Clarity.* This dimension refers to the way in which policies, procedures, and responsibilities are defined and carried out. Early childhood workers at centers scoring high on this dimension generally feel that communication is good and that work schedules, job descriptions, and rules are clear and well defined. Low ratings on this dimension indicate that people often are confused about policies and procedures and that conflicting demands often are placed on workers.

*Reward system.* This dimension measures the extent to which individuals in the setting feel that pay and fringe benefits are fair and equitably distributed. Centers scoring high in this category provide good job security for their workers and handle promotions and raises fairly. Workers in these settings feel that their pay is fair compared to what other early childhood centers pay and that their center is taking steps to improve the overall level of pay and benefits. A low score in this dimension indicates that people may feel that some individuals are paid more than they are worth, that raises are based on favoritism, and that people are taken advantage of.

*Decisionmaking.* This dimension refers to the extent to which autonomy is valued and staff are encouraged to make decisions about those things that directly affect them. Centers scoring high in this category are those where staff are also encouraged to provide input on schoolwide policies. A low rating on this dimension indicates that the overall perception of workers is that the center values conformity and individuals do not feel free to express their opinions on important issues.

*Goal consensus.* The dimension of goal consensus refers to the degree to which staff agree on school philosophy, are unified in their approach, and are committed to program goals and objectives. A high score in this area reflects the ability of staff to appreciate differing points of view and compromise or agree on important programmatic issues. A low rating on this dimension indicates a lack of consistency and agreement on key philosophical issues guiding center practices.

*Task orientation.* This dimension measures the degree of emphasis placed on good planning, efficiency, and getting the job done. Workers who rate their center high in this area believe that they work hard but still have time to relax, that program procedures are efficient, and that meetings are productive. Low ratings generally indicate that time is often wasted, things get put off, and people often procrastinate about getting important tasks done.

*Physical setting.* This dimension measures the extent to which staff feel that their work environment is well arranged, is organized, and provides sufficient supplies and equipment for them to do their jobs. A low score in this category indicates that the center may appear drab or need major repairs, that the temperature may be too hot or too cold, that parking may be inadequate, or that classroom space is cramped and crowded.

*Innovativeness.* This final dimension measures the extent to which the center encourages staff to be creative and innovative in their work. Individuals rating their setting high in this area believe that they are encouraged to try out new ideas in problem solving and are then supported in implementing needed changes. Programs rating low in this dimension are characterized by a traditional approach that avoids risk and allows many problems to go unaddressed.

***Part B. Summary of Worker Values.*** People do not all want or expect the same things from their work environment. For some individuals a sense of collegiality may be quite important and essential for job satisfaction. For others who prefer to work alone, the need for affiliation may be less important. Likewise, for some people the comfort level of the physical setting and the availability of materials and supplies may be of considerable importance. For others, however, the physical setting may be minimally important.

On page 3 of the ECWES, respondents are asked to place a *3* next to the three dimensions they value most highly in a work setting. The Work Environment Profile summarizes the collective importance or value that staff have assigned to each of the ten dimensions. It notes the number of employees who indicated a dimension as being one of the three most important to them.

The data summarized in Part B of the Work Environment Profile can guide the director in knowing which dimensions should be given high priority in terms of change. In other words, administrators will achieve more lasting results in their school improvement efforts if they focus on those areas that staff rated as low in Part A and valued as high in Part B. Looking at parts A and B together will help staff members appreciate the uniqueness of their setting. Part A describes the climate as it is currently perceived by staff; Part B measures the value or importance attached to each dimension. Taken together, Part A and Part B can help staff understand how the current climate meets expectations in each area. Each center must develop its own formula for achieving a healthy organizational climate; no one prescription applies equally to all settings.

***Part C. Summary of Overall Commitment to the Organization.*** This scale provides a summary of the staff's overall commitment to the center. Individuals who feel deeply committed to their jobs tend to put extra effort into their work and take pride in their center. This section of the profile can be read like a thermometer. The higher the bar, the stronger the collective commitment of those individuals completing the survey.

***Part D. Summary of How Current Work Environment Resembles Ideal.*** Satisfaction with one's work environment can also be conceptualized as the discrepancy between current working conditions and a perceived "ideal" work environment. Satisfaction is greater when the discrepancy between real and ideal conditions is small. This section of the Work Environment Profile describes the composite employee perceptions of how closely their current work situation resembles their ideal work environment. This is just one additional way to understand how workers perceive present work conditions.

***Part E. Ranking of Various Educational Goals and Objectives.*** There are many educational goals and objectives that guide curricular policies and procedures in early childhood programs. But the priority that staff assign to different goals may vary from one center to another. This section of the Work Environment Profile details the rank that respondents assigned to six different educational objectives. If goal consensus is high at a center, the rankings for each objective will cluster.

***For some people a collegial work environment is key to job satisfaction; for other people professional growth, supervisor support, or other factors are more important.***

If staff have strong differences in the importance of different objectives, however, the rankings will be widely dispersed.

***Part F. Degree of Decisionmaking Influence of the Teaching Staff.*** This section of the Work Environment Profile describes workers' perceptions regarding the degree of influence that teaching staff have with respect to various organizational decisions. It includes workers' perceptions of the degree of *current* decisionmaking influence of teachers as well as their perceptions of their *desired* degree of decisionmaking influence.

The data summarized in this section of the profile may prove useful in understanding some of the different decisions that are typically made in early childhood programs—both those where centralized decisionmaking may be preferred and those where shared decisionmaking may be possible. The appropriate balance for each center will depend on the unique set of circumstances within each program and the amount of influence desired by staff in each of these areas.

## WHAT IS THE "BEST" CLIMATE?

Healthy, positive organizational climates are typically characterized by high energy, openness, trust, a collective sense of the ability to get things done, and a shared vision of mission. In contrast, an unhealthy, negative environment usually can be described as having poor communication, divisiveness, conflict, and low staff morale.

Nevertheless, each center must define its own "best" professional climate. Just as some of us prefer hot, dry weather and others of us like it cool and damp, the social-ecological perspective discussed earlier helps us understand that there is no one ideal profile. Rather, each dimension must be evaluated in relation to the needs, values, and expectations of the workers and, if applicable, the board members or managers within each setting. The best climate will be a unique blend that meets the individual and collective needs of all concerned.

Conducting a survey about organizational climate is not an end in itself but rather the first stepping-stone toward action. Simply assessing attitudes is not sufficient to increase staff morale and commitment to organizational goals. Diagnosis and evaluation of results lend direction for you to take action.

# 3

# *Different Roles, Different Perceptions*

## DIRECTORS AND TEACHERS VIEW THE WORLD DIFFERENTLY

Any teacher who has worked her way up the ranks from classroom assistant to teacher to director will not be surprised to learn that individuals who hold different positions in the organizational hierarchy tend to view organizational climate differently. In most work settings, those in managerial positions tend to view the agency more positively than do their assistants.

Research conducted at the elementary and secondary levels has found that teachers' and principals' perceptions of school climate do not necessarily coincide. Teachers and administrators have different frames of reference and, consequently, different perceptions of school problems (Fox 1974; Sweeney 1980; Anderson 1982). Principals tend to view conditions more favorably than do teachers. Although teachers and principals generally agree on which problems are serious, they differ considerably in their perceptions of the magnitude of those problems (Reineke & Welch 1975; Sandefur & Smith 1980).

One might assume that early childhood work environments would be different. In elementary and secondary educational settings, a hierarchical model prevails where the delineation

***Administrators and teachers cannot assume that they see the program climate the same way.***

of titles, roles, and corresponding job duties is highly differentiated. In contrast, early childhood educators have long prided themselves on creating educational settings that are more egalitarian and participatory in nature, where shared space, shared responsibilities, and frequent interaction between teachers and administrators is the rule of thumb.

In many early childhood settings, program directors report that they wear many hats, managing the "business" aspects of the program but also spending considerable time working directly with children alongside their teachers. Classroom aides, teachers, and directors often engage in the same duties, despite differences in their job titles. Given these overlapping domains of responsibility, it might be expected that teachers and directors would share similar perceptions of organizational climate.

Apparently this is not the case. As Figure 2 dramatically illustrates, teachers and administrators in early childhood settings have strong differences in perceptions about organizational practices (Bloom 1996b).

A comparison of directors' and teachers' responses to individual items measured on the Early Childhood Work Environment Survey promotes understanding of how individuals in different roles view

***Figure 2.***

**A Comparison of Administrators' and Teachers' Perceptions of Organizational Climate**

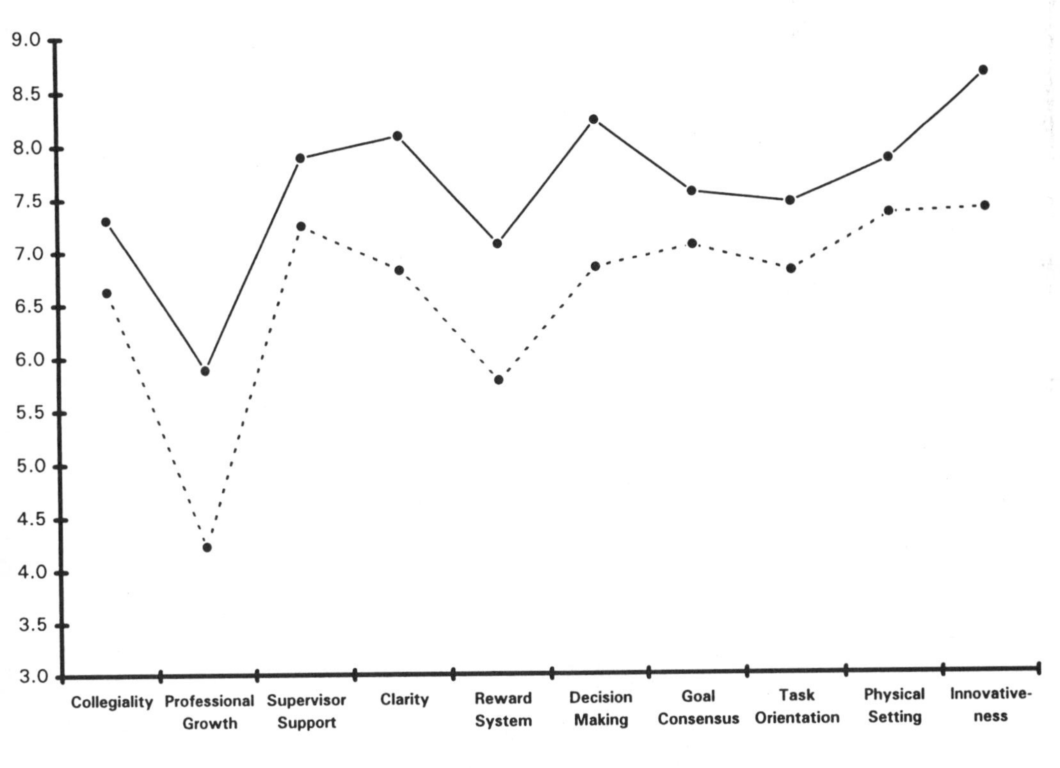

the world. Figure 3 summarizes directors' and teachers' perceptions regarding different organizational practices as measured on two of the subscales of the ECWES—decisionmaking and reward system. (The category of "teachers" in this graph includes both teachers and assistant teachers.) It is clear from the data summarized in these graphs that directors consistently have a rosier picture of organizational practices than do their teachers.

Why is this so? Probably several complex and interrelated factors are at work, including differences in the backgrounds of the two groups, the scope and nature of the roles of each, and the perceived control that directors and teachers have over their jobs.

If we look at the background characteristics of administrators and teachers in early childhood programs, for example, we find significant differences in age, education, experience, salary, and professional orientation. These differences may help explain why administrators and teachers perceive the same environment differently. Rogers (1995) uses the term *heterophily* to describe the existence of differences between groups of individuals. He points out that as groups become more *homophilious,* communication and understanding between them increases.

The scope and nature of the administrative and teaching roles directly relates to the way time is allocated. The assumption that teachers and directors in child care centers are in close contact and share similar experiences by their overlapping roles may be a flawed one. While the research in this area is limited, at least one study supports this conclusion. In his analysis of 35 child care centers in New England, Neugebauer (1975) found that 83% of the directors spent no time working directly with children on a regular basis. Forty-three percent of the teachers in these centers felt that the director was not in "close touch" with what was happening in the classroom. Perhaps the roles of director and teacher are more distinct than was previously assumed.

Clearly, role differentiation is closely tied to perceived control. This may be why administrators as a group perceive organizational climate more favorably than do their staff. In addition to the items noted in Figure 3, teachers also more often state that "the director

*Figure 3.*

## A Comparison of Directors' and Teachers' Responses to Items on Two ECWES Subscales

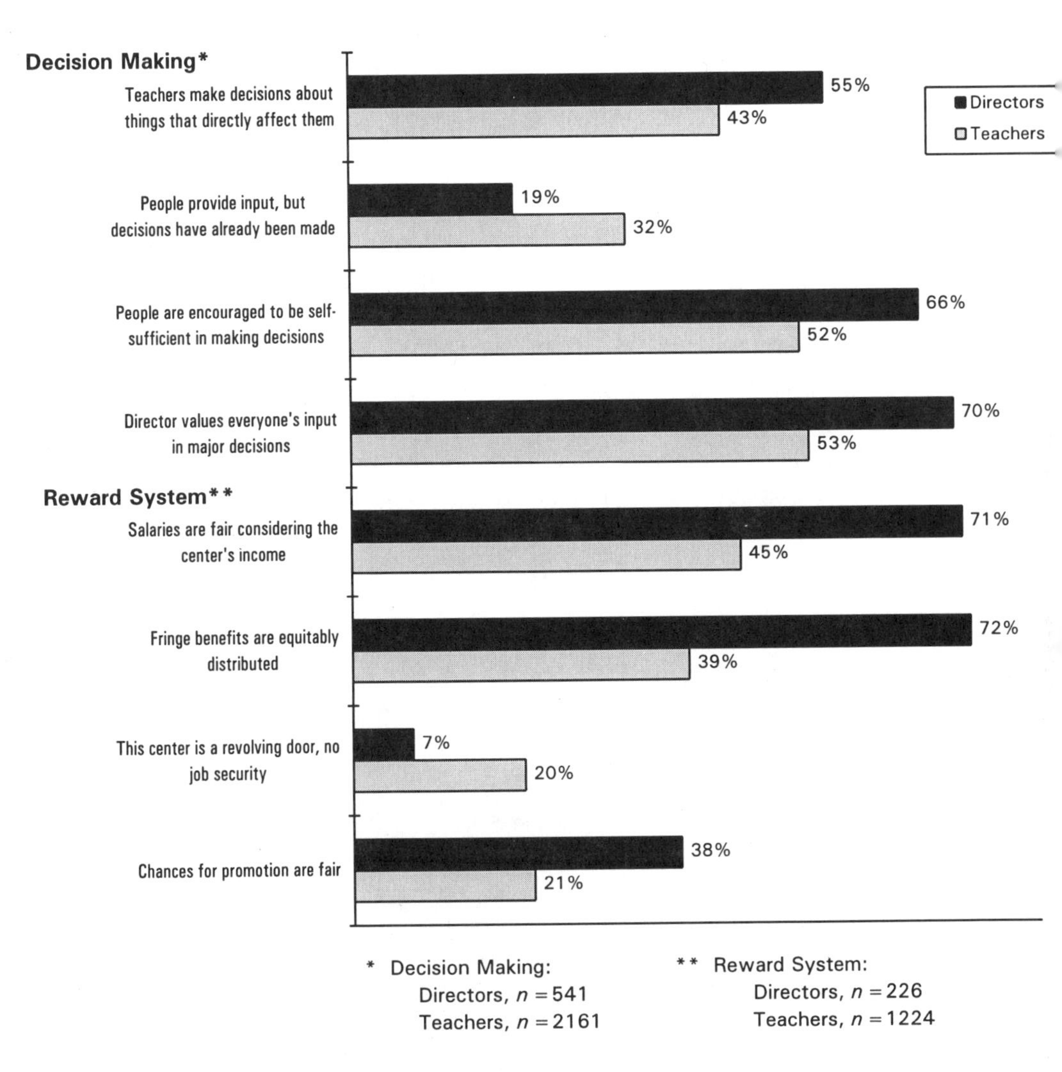

likes to make most of the decisions" and "teachers are seldom asked their opinion on issues."

Whitebook and her associates (1982) found that teachers often have little power or control in making decisions affecting center life. On paper the decisionmaking structure of a program may look quite egalitarian; in reality, however, teachers perceive a strong hierarchical arrangement.

This observation is also supported by Neugebauer's (1975) research. He found that teachers consistently rated decisionmaking more authoritarian than did directors. Fifty percent of the teachers in the large centers he surveyed and 42% of those in small centers indicated that major decisions were made by directors without consultation with teachers.

Data from research using the Early Childhood Work Environment Survey substantiates this view (Bloom 1996b). As seen in Figure 4, more than 75% of the full-time teaching staff from 421 centers report that they have less decisionmaking influence than they would like. Only 6% indicate that they actually have more decisionmaking responsibility than they would like, and less than 20% of the teaching

***Figure 4.***

**Teachers' Perceptions of Their Overall Decisionmaking Influence (*N* = 2161 full-time teaching staff from 421 centers)**

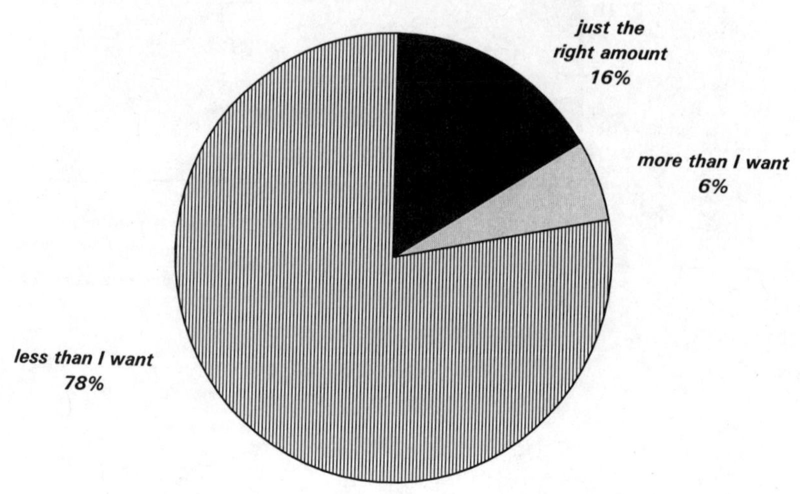

staff say they have "just the right amount." Clearly, there are strong differences in perceptions with respect to influence and control regarding decisionmaking in early childhood programs.

## CLOSING THE GAP

What does this mean for directors interested in improving the climate of their centers? Foremost, it suggests that administrators and teachers cannot assume that their view of center life is necessarily a shared one. Whether differences in perceptions arise from differences in background, the structure of roles and responsibilities, or the perceived control associated with those roles, it is clear that individuals do "filter" their perceptions of organizational practices depending on their position in the center.

A mismatch between directors' and teachers' perceptions can have a detrimental effect on the quality of work life for staff. Identifying where perceptions differ is an important first step in beginning to structure opportunities to promote convergence in viewpoints. Recognizing that people have differing viewpoints can help individuals become sensitive to the reasons for these differences and the impact they can have on program functioning.

As a profession, we have long championed the importance of promoting diversity and appreciating individual differences in our early childhood programs. Indeed, one of NAEYC's best-selling publications is *Anti-Bias Curriculum: Tools for Empowering Young Children* (Derman-Sparks & the A.B.C. Task Force 1989), a book devoted to helping individuals become more tolerant and accepting of those who are different. We need to take this same mind-set into the managerial and staff relations arena of program operations. Respecting differing perceptions of our work world is an important step toward promoting the kind of center climate that truly values diversity.

# 4

# Ways to Improve your Program's Work Climate

## THE DIRECTOR'S ROLE IN ORGANIZATIONAL CHANGE

The director's role in the early childhood organization is both central and complex. In a number of powerful ways, the director shapes the center as a workplace. The director as leader plays a pivotal role in both assessing current work attitudes and structuring changes to improve conditions.

Directors of programs where quality-of-work-life issues are central demonstrate the qualities of effective leadership in their work daily. They have a clear, informed vision of what they want their center to become. They know how to translate that vision into realistic goals and expectations for their board, teachers, parents, and children. They know how to establish a climate that supports progress toward those goals and expectations. And, most importantly, they know how to intervene in a supportive manner when change is necessary.

This kind of leadership does not just happen. You must carve out a leadership role that makes quality-of-work-life issues a central priority. More than any other individual, you are the change agent that can have the greatest impact on your school's organizational climate.

Change is not something that can be forced or imposed. Rather, it should be a process whereby you work with your board and teachers in a collaborative partnership to achieve common goals. If staff are actively involved in assessing the climate of the center, they are more apt to support recommended changes.

There is no quick and simple way to change the climate of an early childhood center. Behaviors and attitudes may be firmly entrenched. The assessment process, however, is a beginning because it engages staff in the common task of evaluating their own work environment. The nonverbal message of the process is a powerful one: The responsibility to improve the quality of work life is shared.

Two-way communication can be improved through the assessment process when people feel that their opinions and ideas are valued. When both staff and leadership perceive the results of the survey as valid, accurate, and unbiased, the description of organizational conditions can be a potent force in helping bring about needed change.

You have started the cycle of change just by reading this book and perhaps by preparing to survey perceptions about the work environment in your own program. As you and your staff begin together to solve small, manageable problems, you will also be achieving something much larger. You will be establishing and reinforcing a norm of continuous improvement in your center—a central principle of Total Quality Management. When teachers are consulted, their ideas taken seriously, and their concerns heard, the channels of communication open and isolating barriers lower.

## SOME QUESTIONS TO THINK ABOUT

How can directors more effectively promote a positive professional climate in their early childhood centers? The following questions are intended as a framework to help you translate the dimensions of organizational climate into action.

### How is staff collegiality encouraged?

People who enter the child care field usually are caring and compassionate people. But the treadmill of activity that consumes their time and energy on the job often keeps them from establishing close relationships with one another. The physical layout of space, time pressures, and conflicting schedules are just some of the barriers that prevent staff from exchanging information, sharing ideas, and lending and receiving support.

The director plays an instrumental role in encouraging staff to support one another. But wise administrators know they cannot force a sense of esprit de corps. Contrived collegiality invariably backfires. A sense of community must be nurtured and developed by careful attention to the social and affiliation needs of the people who work together. You can therefore enhance collegiality by structuring opportunities that enable teachers to work collaboratively on projects, share resources, and solve problems together.

Some centers begin each staff meeting with a few minutes for teachers to informally share a new resource or curriculum idea with others. Other directors ask two or more teachers to work together on a special project, such as a parent meeting or end-of-the-year picnic.

***Collegiality can be enhanced if structured opportunities enable teachers to work collaboratively on projects, share resources, and solve problems together.***

Scheduling can play a big part in fostering collegiality. Perhaps some teachers can be assigned blocks of time to work together to develop new classroom materials or plans for future activities. You might adjust work hours to encourage joint field trips, the sharing of curriculum materials among classrooms, or even carpooling. Shared lunch or coffee breaks can also be a time to informally encourage teamwork.

A staff lounge can work wonders to promote team spirit. Even a small room gives teachers their own space to meet, prepare materials, and talk to one another without disruption. Hang a bulletin board in a visible place so staff can exchange information about teaching ideas and materials. Keep your staff roster up-to-date, and distribute or post a staff birthday list—two seemingly small but very important steps to building collegiality.

If staffing patterns, layout, or time pressures make it difficult for staff to get together during the day, you may need to find time before or after work for people to socialize. Some directors hold regular potluck breakfasts or dinners. Others host a happy hour on Friday afternoons so staff can talk about the good things that happened during the week. Still others schedule an annual weekend retreat during the summer where staff can get together (without their spouses and children) to establish and renew relationships.

New staff need special attention during their first few days to assure that they feel comfortable in their work environment. Welcome them warmly as part of the family; explain the simple details, such as where to get a cup of coffee; and introduce them to everyone—other staff, the children, and, of course, the parents. Plan a systematic way to cover information that new staff need to know during the first day, the first week, and the first month of their employment (Weinstein & Allen 1985). Experienced teachers can take an active role in orienting new teachers.

## What opportunities are provided for professional development?

Providing ample opportunities for professional development is important in any educational setting, but it is particularly crucial in the early childhood field, where directors must often hire caregivers who have had little or no prior training. As the demand for caregiv-

***A good program weaves professional growth into the daily life of the center at little or no cost.***

ers continues to escalate, directors will increasingly be called upon to provide on-the-job training for unskilled workers (Shirah, Hewitt, & McNair 1993). The provision of professional development must not be haphazard; too much is at stake.

Even on a limited budget, there are many ways you can increase opportunities for staff to expand their knowledge base and develop new skills and competencies. When professionalism is promoted, teachers engage in frequent, continuous, and precise talk about teaching practices. They plan, design, research, prepare, and evaluate teaching materials together. But more importantly, they are encouraged to regularly reflect on their performance, evaluate feedback, and examine new and alternative practices (Little 1982).

Some programs provide release time for teachers to observe master teachers in action or to go to a local teachers' center to make new materials. Others pay registration fees for staff to attend workshops or professional conferences. Not only do these activities rejuvenate teachers but the benefits multiply when teachers return and share new information and resources with other staff.

Many directors feel as if they do not have the financial resources to hire substitutes when staff are gone or to pay for inservice specialists to come in to do training. But the amount of support that different centers give to professional development activities seems to be tied more to managerial priorities than to real financial limitations. Some centers with limited financial resources have very strong professional development programs.

Professional growth opportunities need not be limited to special occasions. Instead, a good program weaves professional growth into the daily life of the center at little or no cost by

- encouraging teachers to share information regarding instructional methods and materials;
- setting aside time at staff meetings for each person to share expertise in areas such as child development or classroom management;
- inviting professors from local colleges to talk about their research or specialty;
- encouraging teachers to observe one another and work together to improve teaching practices; and
- maintaining a professional library where staff can read books, journals, or brochures and view videotapes dealing with different areas of early childhood education.

One of the most important ways a director can help motivate teachers is to provide opportunities for them to expand and improve their repertoire of teaching skills. The more skilled teachers are, the more likely they are to experience—and be rewarded by—incidents of success (Neugebauer 1984). The director's role is one of helping teachers identify their specific training needs and of providing proper resources. These resources may be in the form of books and materials, coaching and on-site supervision, inservice training, or outside workshops and courses.

NAEYC has developed guidelines that can serve as a framework for thinking about the professional skill building of practitioners (Willer 1994). This model of professional development delineates a career lattice and the essential core knowledge that practitioners in early childhood programs need to be effective in their roles.

The key to successful staff development is individualizing training needs to the experiential level and career stage of each worker (Hinson, Caldwell, & Landrum 1989; Bloom, Sheerer, & Britz 1991). The underlying assumption in this view is that teachers progress personally and professionally along a developmental path. Each stage has characteristics that make it distinct from preceding and subsequent levels. The kinds of concerns, capabilities, and perspectives that teachers have at one stage are not the same as those of teachers with different levels of experience and training. Single-approach training will work for some but not all staff. If professional development is to be meaningful, it must be tailored to the needs of individual teachers.

There are five resources that will help you get started in your task of developing a master plan for addressing the professional development needs of each of your staff. Carter and Curtis's book *Training Teachers: A Harvest of Theory and Practice* (1994) contains a wealth of practical training ideas for improving the knowledge, skills, and competencies of caregivers. *Blueprint for Action: Achieving Center-Based Change Through Staff Development* (Bloom, Sheerer, & Britz 1991) provides guidelines for developing a career ladder for your center and a number of training assessment tools for individualizing staff-development opportunities for teachers with different levels of education and experience. *Essentials,* edited by Carol Brunson Phillips (1991), describes what competent teachers of young children do. This book serves as a wonderful guide for training CDA candidates. Diane Trister Dodge's *A Guide for Supervisors and Trainers on Implementing the Creative Curriculum* (1993) provides detailed instructions and sample handouts for workshops on different curriculum areas. Finally, *The Early Childhood Mentoring Curriculum,* published by the Center for the Child Care Workforce (1996), is an excellent guide for those interested in setting up an effective mentoring system.

When setting up a comprehensive plan for professional development for a center, it is essential to remember that teachers vary in their receptivity to learning new ideas. Joyce and Showers (1988) have characterized teachers as omnivores, active consumers, passive consumers, resistant, and withdrawn. They argue that more attention should be given to matching different types of teachers with staff-development programs appropriate to their varying appetites for learning.

***When teachers' jobs are designed to make the most of the intrinsic enjoyment they receive from their work, their job satisfaction and group morale are high.***

Directors also serve as role models of professionalism, in and out of the classroom. Although you may not be involved with the children every day, by making it a point to be warm and inviting with the children and their families, you demonstrate your ability to listen to children and parents as well as to teachers. Readily pitching in to assist during a sudden staff shortage, a field trip, or other immediate need for assistance gives you opportunities to demonstrate skilled interactions with children and other staff.

Your active involvement in professional organizations indicates your commitment to your own growth and sets an example for what is expected of staff. Some centers pay membership fees for teachers to belong to the National Association for the Education of Young Children, the Association for Childhood Education International (ACEI), or other similar groups to help ensure a commitment to and a continuity of professional development. Gift subscriptions to professional journals often are given for birthdays or employment anniversary dates.

When you get involved in advocacy activities in your community, teachers will begin to internalize your efforts as part of their own professional repertoire. Some centers set the standard of excellence for good early childhood education in their community because their staff have consistently been such strong, visible supporters of quality services for children and their families.

Once professional development opportunities are supported, they gather momentum as teachers learn about more varied ways in which they can learn from each other and from other experts in the field.

## What types of regular feedback do teachers get about their performance?

Peter Drucker reminds us that people are not machines. "Machines can be worked," says Drucker, "humans must be developed" (1977, 58). This distinction is critical to educational programs because of its implication for the way directors tap into the intrinsic motivation of staff. An integral part of the director's leadership role is helping teachers build opportunities for enrichment and personal achievement.

All of us need to know we are valued for our hard work. When you give your staff open, honest, and regular feedback, you lay the foundation for respect and feelings of self-worth. You can help make individuals aware of what they do well and inspire them to improve their performance in areas that are weak.

How do you go about this? Your approach will be most effective if you structure your performance appraisal so that you and the teacher work in concert to generate solutions and explore alternatives. Concentrate on the teacher's behavior rather than on personality traits. Make your feedback specific rather than global, and focus on the future rather than dwell on the past. Regular, open communication of this kind helps staff grow both personally and professionally. Feedback is the mortar that cements professional relationships in any early childhood program.

Teachers are their own best source of motivation (Neugebauer 1984). If teachers' jobs are designed in such a way as to maximize the intrinsic enjoyment they receive from their work, then directors have made an important stride in increasing individual job satisfaction and group morale.

Central in the motivation equation is the ability of the director to tailor his or her supervisory style to the developmental level of the teacher (Caruso & Fawcett 1986). We take for granted the concept of developmental appropriateness when we think about our interactions with children, but we often forget that the same principle applies to adult supervisory and mentor relationships (Cassidy & Myers 1993; Vartuli & Fyfe 1993). Supervisory practices should vary depending on the career stage, degree of professional competence, and level of commitment of each teacher. For some teachers this might entail a very directive approach. For others it will mean a collaborative or nondirective approach (Glickman 1985).

Another mechanism for enhancing teacher motivation is to help teachers structure their jobs so that they have more opportunities to experience achievement, recognition, advancement, and competence. Too often we look at job descriptions and try to mold the person to a particular role. But real stretching of human resources comes from looking at the individual first and defining the job around that person.

Many directors schedule a joint planning conference with each staff member twice a year. The purpose of this session is to work together to outline the teacher's individual professional goals and to evaluate performance. These one-on-one conferences breathe life into a job description and enable you as director to facilitate each teacher's professional growth.

All of us, including teachers, need change. This idea is summed up perfectly by Selye, who notes, "The human body, like tires on a car, wears longest when it wears evenly" (1976, 433). Variety, new challenges, and opportunities help us develop a broader range of interests and skills.

The joint planning conference, therefore, can be a source of new ways to keep staff challenged and involved. Rotating jobs so staff members do different tasks on a regular basis enriches positions, as does increasing responsibilities, scope, importance, visibility, or challenge. Enriching jobs is a powerful stimulus to increase teachers' self-motivation.

Personal goals differ with each staff member, so job enrichment strategies that appeal to one person may not entice another. Job enrichment incentives must be consistent with each person's goals and work values.

It is usually a good idea to schedule your individual planning conferences just before the new term begins in the fall, as this is when staff changes often take place, schedules shift, and many new children enroll. Select another time for a second conference in the middle of the year to measure accomplishments, evaluate performance, and refine goals.

## How well are roles and responsibilities defined?

In many early childhood settings, jobs have a way of mushrooming out of control, with task after task piling upon an already ambiguous job description. Ill-defined job responsibilities are frustrating and stressful. Confusion and conflict can result from lack of clarity about who is supposed to do what.

Teachers and assistants often work together as a team and share a range of responsibilities. As we have seen, in many programs neither job titles, salaries, nor educational levels distinguish the type of work you might find any staff member doing, although the amount of time spent on a task or type of task might vary among assistants, teachers, head teachers, and even directors. There are always spills to be wiped up, activities to be prepared, field trips to be arranged, and parent meetings to be planned.

Directors need to periodically reexamine the structure of job designations so that job titles are based on skill and experience differences. NAEYC's Model of Professional Development can serve as a guide for conceptualizing different roles in the early childhood setting (Willer 1994). In addition, employees need to have a clear understanding of the limits of their work. They need to know not only what they are expected to do but also what they are not expected to do. Teachers who work within specific role expectations feel more secure about their ability to perform their functions effectively.

Beyond role expectations, center policies and procedures also need to be clearly articulated. Personnel policies pertaining to sick leave, absenteeism, maternity or paternity leave, grievance procedures, teacher preparation time, and expectations for teacher involvement in center fundraising functions need to be put in writing and explained to new staff before they are hired. There are many excellent resources to guide directors in the writing of different center policies as they relate to these staff issues (Travis & Perreault 1981; Perreault 1989; Sciarra & Dorsey 1995). Other policies, for example those regarding sick children, first aid, administration of medicine, parent visits, transportation, field trips, fee payments, snacks and meals, and permission slips, should be put in writing as well to ensure that teachers understand what is expected of them in each of these situations.

Clarity is achieved also by effective communication systems, particularly the way in which information is disseminated. At centers where communication channels are weak, teachers often remark that they are the last to know about a new procedure or an event that has been planned. They say that they receive too many memos and notes, so they do not know which ones are important. They complain that they are bombarded with too much verbal information when they are at staff meetings or when they are preoccupied doing something else. Directors of these programs often find themselves repeating directions several times and feeling frustrated when important information has been miscommunicated.

The first step to improving communication in a program is to assess how information is filtered both vertically and horizontally through the center. Once this is done, directors often find it easier to devise more streamlined methods of communication that highlight important information on a regular and anticipated basis. Essential to this task is determining what kind of information is best communicated in verbal form and what kind is best disseminated in written form. Protecting staff and parents from information overload is important in an age when computers and photocopy machines have made it easy to generate mountains of letters, memos, and reports in very little time. It is easy to get buried under a paper avalanche.

Creating a system where certain kinds of written information are communicated in a regular and anticipated way is the first step to coping with clutter. For example, some directors distribute a Monday morning memo (printed on the same color of paper to distinguish it from the other notes teachers get) that summarizes important information that teachers need to know for the week (e.g., field trips planned, forms due, observations scheduled). Sending out the center newsletter on the same day each month is a way to enable parents to anticipate communication in a predictable way.

## How fair and equitable is the reward system? How well does it promote job security?

Virtually every study examining teacher job satisfaction in early childhood education indicates that child care workers are dissatisfied with the low pay and paltry benefits they receive. Teachers' salaries have never been high, but the situation seems to be worsening because salaries have not kept pace with inflation.

Why do low salaries continue to exist in such an important field? There are a number of complicated reasons, including wage discrimination against females, the labor-intensive nature of early childhood programs, the fact that until recently many mothers provided child care at no cost, the relatively low incomes of young families, and the reality that our culture is not child centered (Modigliani 1986).

Demanding working conditions that include inadequate wages and meager benefits make it difficult—if not impossible—to attract and retain good staff, and program quality suffers as a result. Salaries and benefits are tied into the complex problem of how to fund good early childhood programs.

The issue has now reached crisis proportions in the United States, with severe staff shortages and inadequate attention to safety and learning as the result. The outcry about this intolerable situation has been growing due in large part to the support from organizations including the Center for the Child Care Workforce, the National Association for the Education of Young Children, the Child Care Action Campaign, and other advocacy and professional groups. Every director should be involved in these national efforts to upgrade the profession and thus the quality of early childhood programs for all children.

In your own community, you can begin by surveying other nearby programs about their salaries, benefits, and promotion schedules. Regularly review your policies, and keep your staff informed about what is happening to improve conditions in your program.

Salaries at the early childhood level will undoubtedly remain low for the foreseeable future. But that should not prevent directors from aggressively pursuing other avenues that promote a fair and equitable system of rewards.

People work best when they know the philosophy underlying their pay and their potential for promotion. At a minimum, employees need to understand how decisions are made about salaries and promotions. The key to a good compensation system is both internal fairness (for example, a secretary does not make more than a teacher) and external fairness (a teacher makes a comparable salary to teachers at other centers) (Bloom 1993a, 1993b).

Misunderstandings often can occur when individuals do not have enough information on matters that directly affect their welfare. Many directors have been successful in eliminating the adversarial relationship between administration and staff by being more open about budgetary matters and sharing information regarding fiscal decisions. This need not be full disclosure about where every dollar is spent, but sometimes sharing concerns about the rising cost of insurance and the cost of workers' compensation, disability insurance, and utilities can give staff a greater awareness of the complexities involved in balancing the budget.

The provision of breaks and sick days is certainly related to the adequacy of funds. But the attitude of the director regarding breaks and sick days is critical. Emphasizing the value of teachers' taking

***Even when programs have severely curtailed funds, the director's attitude about salaries, breaks, and sick leave can make a big difference.***

regular breaks and staying home when they are ill can convey to staff that taking advantage of these policies does not mean lack of commitment to their jobs. With creative scheduling, adjustments can enable workers to have additional time to prepare materials and conduct conferences. It is important, also, that policies regarding substitutes do not put a burden on healthy staff. Money for paying substitutes must be budgeted, and staff should be encouraged to use their sick days when they need to. Some centers have replaced the term *sick days* with a more open policy of *mental health days*.

Many directors endorse a policy of differential pay based on merit. This conveys to teachers that they will be rewarded for performance and not just "putting in time." Merit increases can be tied to professional development and advanced degrees, as well as to taking on additional responsibilities at the center. Instituting a salary schedule that ensures some degree of job security can also be a strong indicator to staff of the administrator's interest in their welfare (Bloom 1993a, 1993b; Neugebauer 1994).

The notion of advancement being tied to a career ladder has gained considerable attention in recent years. The appealing thing about career ladder proposals is their potential for upgrading the professional orientation of staff. The research on career development of teachers indicates that there are discernible stages in teachers' attainment of competencies, which translate into natural ranks on a career ladder (ATE 1985; Burden 1987; Bloom, Sheerer, & Britz 1991). Well-thought-out career ladders recognize and reward good teaching performance and build in incentives for job enrichment and expanded responsibilities.

Some centers have experimented with a variety of fringe benefit plans that are less expensive and easier to implement than increasing salaries across the board for all employees. These benefits include free or reduced tuition for children of employees, reimbursement for courses taken for professional improvement, release time to visit other schools and attend conferences, free lunches, use of the school car, and paid membership fees to professional organizations (Whitebook et al. 1990).

Monetary rewards are not the only way a program's administration can convey respect for its staff. Even after solutions are found to help pay for good early childhood programs in the United States, nonmonetary rewards will continue to be essential.

Administrators know how important it is to respect teachers every day in even the smallest matters. The positive tone you set in your center will be picked up by parents and visitors from the community. You will also want to publicly recognize outstanding performance, perhaps through an annual awards program, a special display honoring a teacher's exceptional service, or recognition at a parent/staff meeting.

Directors who are concerned about the welfare of their teachers are proactive in advocating for higher wages and benefits. They provide parents with information about the full cost of quality, particularly how teachers' low salaries help make it possible for the center to have affordable tuition rates (Zinsser 1986; Willer 1991; NAEYC 1993, 1995).

Concerned directors also encourage staff to get involved in national advocacy efforts, such as the Worthy Wage Campaign, which are designed to educate legislators and the public at large about the importance and cost of high-quality child care and the need for public policies that will improve the status of the early childhood workforce (CCEP 1992; CCDECE 1993). The Center for the Child Care Workforce, the National Association for the Education of Young Children, and the Center for Career Development in Early Care and Education (CCDECE) at Wheelock College are three organizations whose publications will be helpful in this regard.

## How involved are staff in making decisions on important issues?

An integral part of a healthy organizational climate is an uncompromising respect for the need of people to have some say in the decisions that directly affect them. Whether the decision concerns curriculum, furniture arrangement, schedules for parent conferences, or field trip sites, teachers need to have input. When involvement is broadened, directors usually find that staff feel a greater commitment to the program.

It is not easy to involve staff and keep them informed. If you are not already including staff in decisionmaking, you can gradually expand participation by reviewing the range of decisions that are made and the consequences of those decisions (Bloom 1995). In most centers with well-trained teachers, decisions fall into four categories:

1. decisions that are best made by the board or the program director alone *(unilateral decisionmaking)*;
2. decisions that are best made by the director with input by the staff *(consultative decisionmaking)*;
3. decisions that can be made jointly by the director and teachers *(collaborative decisionmaking)*; and
4. decisions that should be made by the teachers or other staff exclusively *(delegated decisionmaking)*. (Bloom 2000, 23)

The level of participation varies according to the expertise, abilities, and interest of the parties involved. Directors sensitive to the importance of staff involvement will want to expand opportunities for staff input through collaborative and delegated decisionmaking. For example, the ordering of materials, the scheduling of rotating responsibilities, and the screening and interviewing of new staff may all involve decisions that could be made collaboratively with teachers.

Participatory management cannot be accomplished overnight. In many cases, behavior patterns and the dynamics of interpersonal relationships are well established, even firmly entrenched. Involvement cannot be thrust on people but must be implemented gradually.

How can you open channels for increased involvement without disrupting your program's continuity? First, you must actively and honestly solicit feedback about how to improve working conditions. Do it formally, through a questionnaire, and informally, as you talk with people every day. So many of us are reluctant to generate feedback and thereby recognize diversity among those with whom we work—even though, as Walter Lippman once remarked, "in organizations where everyone thinks alike, no one thinks very much" (in Schul 1975, 2).

Well-organized staff meetings are another way to ensure that decisionmaking expands. The number of meetings is not nearly as important as the kind of meetings and the degree to which agendas are jointly developed. Staff meetings can become the focal point for building team spirit and a cooperative management approach. When teachers feel comfortable enough to question procedures, suggest alternatives, and exchange different points of view, their morale usually rises.

Do not wait for frustrations to take root and cause job complacency or dissatisfaction. It is best to catch griping and channel it constructively in a way that will improve conditions and increase intrinsic motivation of staff members.

## How are staff involved in setting program goals?

Your role as leader is to develop a shared vision among the staff and board of what you all want the center to become. Much like the conductor of a symphony, the director knows that the combined energy of a group working in harmony creates a whole that is greater than the sum of its parts.

Directors who value the process of collaboration with staff are generally more willing to devote the necessary time to involve staff in setting goals for the program. In the process, teachers will feel that their opinions and suggestions are valued.

There are several guides available to assist directors in crafting a mission statement for their centers (Covey 1989; Barth 1993). Most involve a close examination of core beliefs and values. In the early childhood setting, a mission statement must also be consistent with the center's educational philosophy as it relates to children and families.

Constructing a mission statement that reflects the collective beliefs and values of all involved takes time and patience. The investment of time and energy is well worth it, though.

> An organizational mission statement—one that truly reflects the deep shared vision and values of everyone within that organization—creates a great unity and tremendous commitment. It creates in people's hearts and minds a frame of reference, a set of criteria or guidelines, by which they will govern themselves. (Covey 1989, 143)

A mission statement provides the foundation from which goals and educational objectives can be developed. Goal-setting techniques are varied and include such processes as goal-attainment scaling and

***Key in shaping curriculum experiences for children is periodically collaborating with staff to reassess program objectives.***

values clarification (Bean & Clemes 1978; Glaser 1983). Whatever method is used, it is important that the goals that are agreed upon be realistic and that progress in achieving them can be measured in concrete ways.

The beginning of the school year in September or the start of a new calendar year in January provides a good psychological renewal time to reassess program objectives and develop a series of clear and realistic action steps that will help staff work together to achieve common goals. Having a clear set of purposes that staff agree upon ensures that teachers' efforts will be consistent with the broader mission of the center. A well-formulated goals statement also helps staff set priorities when making decisions about appropriate curriculum experiences for young children. Finally, consensus on goals can reduce teacher anxiety because it provides staff with a kind of benchmark from which to measure progress.

Every director is confronted with urgent business every day, so it is easy to find myriad good excuses to put off the goal-setting process for another year. However, directors who make time for this collaborative process find that it has a broad effect on staff relations. The group's divergent viewpoints merge into a unified, harmonious whole. The self-renewing process helps teachers and administrators strengthen their educational partnership, thus immeasurably improving the quality of education for children.

## How wisely is time used? How realistic are work loads?

Just how does a director create the right balance between professional efficiency and warm informality, between seriousness and silliness, between paperwork and people work, between process and product? To be sure, educating young children is not like building cars; worker productivity cannot be gauged in discrete units, as on an assembly line. But we can use our time wisely to ensure that the center is run both efficiently and effectively and minimizes job-related stress.

Employing a host of time-management strategies is one way to help us begin to use time more wisely (Jorde 1982; Covey, Merrill, & Merrill 1994). For example, one strategy is to do similar tasks—writing letters, filing, making phone calls, or running errands—all at once. Grouping activities allows you to focus your attention and make your day less fragmented.

The director's ability to set priorities, target time, and avoid procrastination certainly has a beneficial impact on staff's ability to perform their jobs well. The director's efficient and effective use of time also serves as a powerful role model for others, particularly for new staff, who may be struggling with how to balance the demands of their personal and professional lives.

Teaching demands an exceptional amount of energy and efficiency, so you should schedule teachers to work when they are at their peak for top performance. Some are morning people, while others begin the most productive part of their day in the afternoon. In addition to schedule considerations, workloads can be juggled to make the best use of time.

Workloads consist of both the sheer quantity of tasks that need to be accomplished and the time frame in which those jobs must be done. Too much to do in too little time (work overload) or too little to do that is stimulating (boredom) are both sources of job stress and can result in lower job satisfaction and performance.

Because people differ in background and training, the trick for administrators is to find the right balance for each person—matching individuals to specific jobs so that they feel challenged and stretched yet not overwhelmed and consumed by too much work pressure. Periodic individual conferences to review each teacher's specific workload, needs, interests, and competencies can demonstrate your respect.

There is another way that directors can show respect for the integrity of those who work for them. They can help staff understand the emotional limits of their work. Being dedicated and loyal to an organization does not mean that teachers must be consumed by their professional obligations. *Dedication does not have to mean deadication.* Indeed, as role models, directors can help employees understand that survival in a profession that demands so much psychic energy depends on our ability to lead a balanced life and look after our own mental health. A certain amount of detachment from one's professional role may be essential to maintaining this healthy perspective. Learning how to emotionally leave one's job at the end of the day is one important way to achieve that perspective.

## How conducive is the physical setting to getting the job done?

Most early childhood environments are designed primarily with the needs of young children in mind. But accommodating staff and parent needs is also an important issue in ensuring a healthy professional work environment (Greenman 1988). A poorly equipped or hastily designed environment can promote tension and frustration.

The physical layout of a program conveys strong nonverbal messages that affect employee and parent perceptions of it. For example, a teacher preparation room sends a strong message that teacher planning is valuable. Likewise, sufficient space to park, a place for personal belongings, and a place to escape during the day for a few minutes of solitude all symbolize how staff are valued and respected.

Issues concerning the use of space in early childhood programs are particularly important because "shared space" is the rule of thumb in most centers. Directors who understand the impact of the physical setting on worker morale find creative ways to make the use of space conducive to achieving their program goals. For example, they ensure that the spatial arrangement allows the administrative functions of the center to be conducted without interfering with program activities. They make sure that staff have a quiet place to conduct a parent conference or have a personal telephone conversation. And they make sure there is sufficient space to store classroom equipment and ample work surfaces to prepare class materials.

Poor arrangement of space can cause a host of potential health and safety hazards (CCEP 1982). Poor lighting, improper ventilation, and high noise levels can make it difficult for teachers to carry out their responsibilities (Makower 1981; Schreiber 1996). Accommodating adult needs in a child-sized environment is not easy. Low counters, small chairs, and child-sized fixtures are essential elements in good programs for young children but may contribute to stress and physical fatigue for the adults who must maneuver in these settings. Staff need time to develop systems to cope with the inevitable daily clutter and a plan to organize furnishings and classroom resources to reduce stress and fatigue.

Select and arrange furniture and fixtures to minimize the incidence of injury, health hazards, and lower-back strain. Check that building materials, insulation, drapes, or carpets do not emit harmful toxins.

Staff and administrators can work closely to evaluate their work environment, make changes, and then review how successful those changes were. Take photos to give yourselves a fresh perspective about the use of your space. Ask preschool or older children in the program for their suggestions. Visit other centers to see what works well. Brush up on the principles of good design. Use graph paper to draw several possible room arrangements before making any major moves. The changes need not be expensive if volunteers are willing to help with carpentry, sewing, painting, or furniture arrangement.

## How are creativity and innovation encouraged?

The only way to unleash the creative energy in an organization is to encourage staff to try new techniques and instructional approaches. Whether teachers are interested in implementing a new perceptual-motor program, integrating microcomputers into the curriculum, or trying out a new classroom management strategy, they need to be supported in their efforts.

Encouragement and support, however, should not be limited to praising successes. Teachers also need to know that occasional setbacks are understood to be part of the change process (Schrag, Nelson, & Siminowsky 1985). In any area of organizational change, the director's attitude is most critical. If the director approaches change with enthusiasm and confidence, that spirit will be conveyed to the staff. The director is the facilitator who carefully paves the way for change, helps keep channels of communication open, and provides support as needed.

Openness to change is not a trait that can be readily measured during the selection process of new staff, but it is a trait that can be nurtured in the right kind of supportive atmosphere. Taking time to consider the reasons for a teacher's resistance to an organizational change is the first step to creating an environment that respects different degrees of openness to new ideas.

Resistance is often based on fear of the unknown. Such anxiety can be alleviated by involving staff as much as possible in the planning and implementation of decisions, keeping them well informed,

***A well-functioning center makes it possible for teachers to enjoy teaching, and they are far less likely to suffer burnout.***

and providing as much time as possible to allow reluctant staff members to psychologically gear up for any impending changes.

Divergent thinking and creativity can also be nurtured by helping staff develop new strategies for looking at old problems. Devoting one staff meeting each month to brainstorming about centerwide problems is one way to unleash creativity, generate new ideas, and share multiple perspectives.

There are a number of wonderful books on the market that are filled with interesting games, puzzles, tips, and techniques for breaking through mental blocks and tapping creative potential (LeBoeuf, 1980; Leff 1984; Adams 1986; von Oech 1990; Buzan 1994). Selecting one of the many exercises or games presented in these books to use at the beginning of each staff meeting will not only be an interesting icebreaker but will also get the staff working together in new, creative ways. These books might also make an ideal birthday present for your teachers.

## IN SUM

Directors of exemplary early childhood programs are like barometers—they constantly assess fluctuations in their organizational climate and they work to make adaptations as necessary. They use the information from formal and informal climate assessment not only to forecast but to shape the climate in which they and their staff work.

Achieving a healthy quality of work life is both a goal and a process—it is something we work toward as well as the means by which we reach that goal. A good climate makes it possible to work effectively to meet the needs of young children and thus achieve our program goals. It also makes the work environment a pleasant place to spend time. The best programs are those that are a great place to work—where teachers and administrators engage jointly in solving problems, making decisions, and implementing changes as needed.

All of us spend a substantial portion of our lives at work. We rely on our employers to be responsible for reducing job-related stress and helping us avoid burnout. All of us deserve to work in environments that use our talents and develop our professional capabilities. As a direct result, the children in our programs benefit.

# REFERENCES


Adams, J.L. 1986. *Conceptual blockbusting.* Reading, MA: Addison-Wesley.

Anderson, C.S. 1982. The search for school climate: A review of the research. *Review of Educational Research* 52 (3): 368–420.

Arnett, J. 1989. Caregivers in day care centers: Does training matter? *Journal of Applied Developmental Psychology* 10: 541–52.

ATE (Association of Teacher Educators). 1985. *Developing career ladders in teaching.* Reston, VA: Author.

Barth, R. 1993. Coming to a vision. *Journal of Staff Development* 4 (1): 6–11.

Bean, R., & H. Clemes. 1978. *Elementary principal's handbook: New approaches to administrative action.* West Nyack, NY: Parker.

Berman, P., & M.W. McLaughlin. 1978. *Federal programs supporting educational change.* Vol. 8, *Implementing and sustaining innovations.* Santa Monica, CA: Rand.

Bloom, P.J. 1993a. "But I'm worth more than that!" Addressing employee concerns about compensation. *Young Children* 48 (3): 65–68.

Bloom, P.J. 1993b. "But I'm worth more than that!" Implementing a comprehensive compensation system. *Young Children* 48 (4): 64–72.

Bloom, P.J. 1995. Shared decisionmaking: The centerpiece of participatory management. *Young Children* 50 (4): 55–60.

Bloom, P.J. 1996a. *Improving the quality of work life in the early childhood setting: Resource guide and technical manual for the Early Childhood Work Environment Survey.* Rev. ed. Wheeling, IL: Early Childhood Development Project, National-Louis University.

Bloom, P.J. 1996b. The quality of work life in early childhood programs: Does accreditation make a difference? In *NAEYC accreditation: A decade of learning and the years ahead,* eds. S. Bredekamp & B. Willer, 13–24. Washington, DC: NAEYC.

Bloom, P.J. 2000. *Circle of influence: Implementing shared decision making and participative management.* Lake Forest, IL: New Horizons.

Bloom, P.J., M. Sheerer, & J. Britz. 1991. *Blueprint for action: Achieving center-based change through staff development.* Lake Forest, IL: New Horizons.

Bowditch J., & A. Buono. 1982. *Quality of work life assessment.* Boston: Auburn House.

Bredekamp, S., & C. Copple, eds. 1997. *Developmentally appropriate practice in early childhood programs.* Rev. ed. Washington, DC: NAEYC.

Bronfenbrenner, U. 1981. *The ecology of human development.* Rev. ed. Cambridge: Harvard University Press.

Bundy, B.F. 1988. Achieving accreditation: A journal of one program's experience. *Young Children* 43 (6): 27–34.

Burden, P. 1987. *Establishing career ladders in teaching.* Springfield, IL: Charles Thomas.

Buzan, T. 1994. *The mind map book.* New York: Dutton.

Carter, M. 1986. NAEYC's center accreditation project: What's it like in real life? *Child Care Information Exchange* 49 (May): 38–41.

Carter, M., & D. Curtis. 1994. *Training teachers: A harvest of theory and practice.* St. Paul, MN: Redleaf.

Caruso, J.J., & M.T. Fawcett. 1986. *Supervision in early childhood education: A developmental perspective.* New York: Teachers College Press.

Cassidy, D., & B.K. Myers. 1993. Mentoring in inservice training for child care workers. *Child & Youth Care Forum* 22 (5): 387–96.

CCDECE (Center for Career Development in Early Care and Education). 1993. *Know your state's financing resources: A guide to funding career development in early care and education.* Boston: Wheelock College.

Center for the Child Care Workforce. 1996. *The early childhood mentoring curriculum.* Washington, DC: Author.

CCEP (Child Care Employee Project). 1982. *Occupational health and safety for child care staff.* Berkeley, CA: Author.

CCEP (Child Care Employee Project). 1992. On the horizon: New policy initiatives to enhance child care staff compensation. *Young Children* 47 (5): 39–42.

Conley, S. 1991. Review of research on teacher participation in school decision making. *Review of Research in Education* 17: 225–66.

Cost, Quality, and Child Outcomes Study Team. 1995. *Cost, quality, and child outcomes in child care centers, public report.* Denver: Economics Department, University of Colorado at Denver.

Coughlan, R.J., & R. Cooke. 1974. Work attitudes. In *Evaluating educational performance,* ed. H.J. Walberg, 295–317. Berkeley, CA: McCutchan.

Covey, S. 1989. *The seven habits of highly effective people.* New York: Simon & Schuster.

Covey, S., A.R. Merrill, & R. Merrill. 1994. *First things first.* New York: Simon & Schuster.

Derman-Sparks, L., & the A.B.C. Task Force. 1989. *Anti-bias curriculum: Tools for empowering young children.* Washington, DC: NAEYC.

Dodge, D.T. 1993. *A guide for supervisors and trainers on implementing the Creative Curriculum.* Washington, DC: Teaching Strategies.

Drucker, P. 1977. *People and performance.* New York: Harper & Row.

Dunn, L. 1995. Influences of the work environment on the caregiving environment in child care. Paper presented at the annual meeting of the American Educational Research Association, San Francisco, April.

Ferrara, D., & T. Repa. 1993. Measuring shared decision making. *Educational Leadership* 51 (2): 71–72.

Fleischer, B. 1985. Identification of strategies to reduce turnover among child care workers. *Child Care Quarterly* 14 (2): 130–39.

Fox, R. 1974. *School climate improvement: A challenge to the school administrator.* Bloomington, IN: Phi Delta Kappa.

Fraser, B.J., G.L. Anderson, & H.L. Walberg. 1982. *Assessment of learning environments: Manual for Learning Environment Inventory (LEI) and My Class Inventory (MCI).* Perth: Western Australian Institute of Technology.

Fullan, M. 1991. *The new meaning of educational change.* New York: Teachers College Press.

Glaser, E. 1983. *Putting knowledge to use.* San Francisco: Jossey-Bass.

Glickman, C.D. 1985. *Supervision of instruction: A developmental approach.* Boston: Allyn & Bacon.

Goodlad, J.I. 1983. The school as workplace. In *Staff development: The eighty-second yearbook of the National Society for the Study of Education,* ed. G.A. Griffin, 36–61. Chicago: University of Chicago Press.

Gottfredson, G.D. 1984. *Using the Effective School Battery.* Odessa, FL: Psychological Assessment Resources.

Greenman, J. 1988. *Caring spaces, learning places: Children's environments that work.* Redmond, WA: Exchange Press.

Griffin, G.A., ed. 1983. *Staff development: The eighty-second yearbook of the National Society for the Study of Education.* Chicago: University of Chicago Press.

Halpin, A.W., & D. Croft. 1963. *The organizational climate of schools.* Chicago: University of Chicago Press.

Herr, J., R.D. Johnson, & K. Zimmerman. 1993. Benefits of accreditation: A study of directors' perceptions. *Young Children* 48 (4): 32–35.

Hinson, S., M. Caldwell, & M. Landrum. 1989. Characteristics of effective staff development programs. *Journal of Staff Development* 10 (2): 48–52.

Howard, E., B. Howell, & E. Brainard. 1987. *Handbook for conducting school climate improvement projects.* Bloomington, IN: Phi Delta Kappa.

Hoy, W., C. Tarter, & R. Kottkamp. 1991. *Open schools/healthy schools: Measuring organizational climate.* London: Sage.

Huseman, R., & J. Hatfield. 1989. *Managing the equity factor.* Boston: Houghton Mifflin.

James, L.R., & A.P. Jones. 1974. Organizational climate: A review of theory and research. *Psychological Bulletin* 81: 1096–1112.

Jones, A.P., & L.R. James. 1979. Psychological climate: Dimensions and relationships of individual and aggregated work environment perceptions. *Organizational Behavior and Human Performance* 23: 201–50.

Jorde, P. 1982. *Avoiding burnout: Managing time, space, and people in early childhood education.* Lake Forest, IL: New Horizons.

Jorde, P. 1984. Change and innovation in early childhood education. Ph.D. diss., Stanford University.

Joyce, B., ed. 1990. *Changing school culture through staff development.* Alexandria, VA: Association for Supervision and Career Development.

Joyce, B., & B. Showers. 1988. *Student achievement through staff development.* New York: Longman.

Joyce W.F., & J.W. Slocum. 1984. Collective climate: Agreement as a basis for defining aggregate climates in organizations. *Academy of Management Journal* 27: 721–42.

Kent, K. 1985. A successful program of teachers assisting teachers. *Educational Leadership* 43 (November): 30–33.

Kontos, S., & A. Stremmel. 1988. Caregivers' perceptions of working conditions in a child care environment. *Early Childhood Research Quarterly* 3 (1): 77–90.

Kozlowski, S., & M. Doherty. 1989. Integration of climate and leadership: Examination of a neglected issue. *Journal of Applied Psychology* 74 (4): 546–53.

LeBoeuf, M. 1980. *Imagineering.* New York: McGraw-Hill.

Lee, M.O., R.M. Buck, & C. Midgley. 1992. The organizational context of personal teaching efficacy. Paper presented at the annual meeting of the American Educational Research Association, San Francisco, April.

Leff, H. 1984. *Playful perception*. Burlington, VT: Waterfront Books.

Lewin, K. 1951. *Field theory in social science*. New York: Harper & Row.

Lightfoot, S. 1983. *Good high schools: Portraits of character and culture*. New York: Basic Books.

Little, J.W. 1982. Norms of collegiality and experimentation: Workplace conditions of school success. *American Educational Research Journal* 19: 325–40.

Makower, J. 1981. *Office hazards: How your job can make you sick*. Tilden Press.

Modigliani, K. 1986. But who will take care of the children? Child care, women, and devalued labor. *Journal of Education* 168 (3): 46–69.

Moos, R.H. 1979. *Evaluating educational environments*. San Francisco: Jossey-Bass.

Moos, R.H. 1986. *The human context*. Rev. ed. Malabar, FL: R. Kriegar.

Morgan, G., S. Azar, J. Costley, A. Genser, I. Goodman, J. Lombardi, & B. McGimsey. 1993. *Making a career of it: The state of the states report on career development in early care and education*. Boston: Wheelock College.

NAEYC (National Association for the Education of Young Children). 1993. *NAEYC position statement for compensation of early childhood professionals*. Washington, DC: Author.

NAEYC (National Association for the Education of Young Children). 1995. *NAEYC position statement on quality, compensation, and affordability*. Washington, DC: Author.

NAEYC (National Association for the Education of Young Children). 1998. *Accreditation criteria and procedures of the National Association for the Education of Young Children—1998 edition*. Washington, DC: Author.

Nash, M. 1983. *Organizational performance*. San Francisco: Jossey-Bass.

Neugebauer, R. 1975. *Organizational analysis of day care*. Cambridge, MA: Lesley College. ERIC, ED 157616.

Neugebauer, R. 1984. Self motivation: Motivation at its best. *Child Care Information Exchange* (October): 7–10.

Neugebauer, R. 1994. Guidelines for fine tuning your salary schedule. *Child Care Information Exchange* (May): 55–64.

Perreault, J. 1989. Developing the employee handbook: Grievance procedure. *Child Care Information Exchange* (April): 41–44.

Pettegrew, L., & G. Wolf. 1982. Validating measures of teacher stress. *American Educational Research Journal* 19 (3): 373–96.

Phillips, C.B., ed. 1991. *Essentials*. Washington, DC: Council for Early Childhood Professional Recognition.

Phyfe-Perkins, E. 1980. Children's behavior in preschool settings—A review of research concerning the influence of the physical environment. In *Current topics in early childhood education,* vol. 3, ed. L. Katz, 91–125. Norwood, NJ: Ablex.

Pope, S., & A. Stremmel. 1992. Organizational climate and job satisfaction among child care teachers. *Child and Youth Care Forum* 21 (1): 39–52.

Powell, I., D. Eisenberg, L. Moy, & J. Vogel. 1994. Costs and characteristics of high quality early childhood education programs. *Child and Youth Care Forum* 23 (2): 103–18.

Prescott, E. 1981. Relations between physical setting and adult/child behavior in day care. In *Advances in early education and day care,* vol. 2, ed. S. Kilmer, 129–58. Greenwich, CT: JAI Press.

Purkey, S.C., & M. Smith. 1982. Too soon to cheer? Synthesis of research on effective schools. *Educational Leadership* 40 (December): 64–69.

Reineke, R., & W. Welch. 1975. Adequacy of teaching conditions as perceived by administrators and teachers. Minneapolis: University of Minnesota. ERIC, ED 161678.

Rogers, E.M. 1995. *Diffusion of innovations*. Rev. ed. New York: Free Press.

Rosenholtz, S. 1989. *Teacher's workplace*. New York: Longman.

Sandefur, W., & H. Smith. 1980. A comparison of the perceptions of classroom teachers and principals in Texas concerning the instructional problems of teachers. *Texas Study of Secondary Educational Research Journal* 25 (1): 11–13.

Schneider, B., & A. Reichers. 1983. On the etiology of climates. *Personnel Psychology* 36 (1): 19–39.

Schrag, L., E. Nelson, & T. Siminowsky. 1985. Helping employees cope with change. *Child Care Information Exchange* (September): 3–6.

Schreiber, M. 1996. Lighting alternatives: Considerations for child care centers. *Young Children* 51 (4): 11–13.

Schul, B. 1975. *How to be an effective group leader*. Chicago: Newson-Hill.

Schwab, R., & E. Iwanicki. 1982. Perceived role conflict, role ambiguity, and teacher burnout. *Review of Educational Research* 18 (1): 60–74.

Sciarra, D.J., & A. Dorsey. 1995. *Developing and administering a child care center.* Albany, NY: Delmar.

Seashore, S.E., E. Lawler, P. Mirvis, & C. Cammann. 1983. *Assessing organizational change.* New York: John Wiley & Sons.

Selye, H. 1976. *Stress of life.* New York: McGraw-Hill.

Sheerer, M., & P.J. Bloom. 1997. Supervision in early childhood education. In *Handbook of research on school supervision,* eds. G. Firth & E. Pajak. New York: Macmillan.

Shirah, S., T. Hewitt, & R. McNair. 1993. Preservice training fosters retention: The case for vocational training. *Young Children* 48 (4): 27–31.

Silver, P., & C. Moyle. 1984. School leadership in relation to school effectiveness. Paper presented at the annual meeting of the American Educational Research Association, New Orleans, April.

Smylie, M. 1992. Teacher participation in school decision making: Assessing willingness to participate. *Educational Evaluation and Policy Analysis* 14 (1): 53–67.

Stremmel, A., M. Benson, & D. Powell. 1993. Communication, satisfaction, and emotional exhaustion among child care center staff: Directors, teachers, and assistant teachers. *Early Childhood Research Quarterly* 8: 221–33.

Stern, D. 1986. Compensation for teachers. *Review of Research in Education* 13: 285–316.

Sweeney, J. 1980. Teacher dissatisfaction on the rise: Higher level needs unfulfilled. *Education* 102: 203–07.

Tagiuri, R. 1978. *The concept of organizational climate.* Ann Arbor, MI: University Microfilm International.

Travis, N., & J. Perreault. 1981. *Day care personnel management.* Atlanta, GA: Save the Children.

Vartuli, S., & B. Fyfe. 1993. Teachers need developmentally appropriate practices too. *Young Children* 48 (4): 6–42.

von Oech, R. 1990. *A whack on the side of the head.* New York: Time Warner.

Weinstein, C. 1979. The physical environment of the school: A review of the research. *Review of Educational Research* 49 (4): 577–610.

Weinstein, M., & J. Allen. 1985. Orienting staff right from the beginning. *Child Care Information Exchange* (March): 1–5.

Whitebook, M., C. Howes, R. Darrah, & J. Friedman. 1982. Caring for the caregivers: Staff burnout in child care. In *Current topics in early childhood education. Vol. 4,* ed. L. Katz, 212–35. Norwood, NJ: Ablex.

Whitebook, M., C. Howes, & D. Phillips. 1989. *Who cares? Child care teachers and the quality of care in America: Final report of the National Child Care Staffing Study.* Berkeley, CA: Child Care Employee Project.

Whitebook, M., C. Pemberton, J. Lombardi, & E. Galinsky. 1990. *From the floor: Raising child care salaries.* Berkeley, CA: Child Care Employee Project.

Whitebook, M., D. Phillips, & C. Howes. 1993. *National child care setting revisited: Four years in the life of center-based child care.* Oakland, CA: Child Care Employee Project.

Wien, C.A. 1995. *Developmentally appropriate practice in "real life": Stories of teacher practical knowledge.* New York: Teachers College Press.

Willer, B., ed. 1991. *Reaching the full cost of quality.* Washington, DC: NAEYC.

Willer, B., ed. 1994. A conceptual framework for early childhood professional development. In *The early childhood career lattice: Perspectives on professional development,* eds. J. Johnson & J.B. McCracken. Washington, DC: NAEYC.

Willer, B., S. Hofferth, E. Kisker, P. Divine-Hawkins, E. Farquhar, & F. Glantz. 1991. *The demand and supply of child care in 1990: Joint findings from the National Child Care Survey 1990 and A Profile of Child Care Settings.* Washington, DC: NAEYC.

Wilson, B., W. Firestone, & R. Herriott. 1984. *The School Assessment Survey: A technical manual.* Philadelphia: Research for Better Schools.

Young, I.P., & K. Kasten. 1980. *The relationship between school climate and implementation of an innovation in elementary school.* Madison: Wisconsin Research and Development Center for Individualized Schooling, University of Wisconsin. ERIC, ED 199925.

Zahorick, J.A. 1984. Cautious colleagues. Paper presented at the annual meeting of the American Educational Research Association, New Orleans, April.

Zigarmi, D. 1981. Leadership and school climate. *Journal of Staff Development* 2: 93–115.

Zinsser, C. 1986. *Day care's unfair burden: How low wages subsidize a public service.* New York: Center for Public Advocacy Research.

# *Appendix A*

## SAMPLE COVER LETTER FOR INFORMAL ASSESSMENT

Date

Dear Staff,

The attached survey is designed to find out how you feel about this center as a place to work. This questionnaire provides you with an opportunity to express your feelings and opinions regarding 10 areas of organizational climate. It also includes some open-ended questions where you may provide some helpful feedback on ways to improve our program. The success of this survey depends on everyone's honest answers. It should take no more than 5 or 10 minutes to complete.

Please know that your answers to these questions are completely confidential. There is no need to put your name on the questionnaire. When you have completed the questionnaire, please put it in the attached envelope, seal it, and give it to ________________. From the tallied results of the questionnaires, we will be able to determine staff's perceptions of program strengths as well as areas that may need improvement.

Thank you for caring enough to share your opinions about these issues. Your cooperation and assistance are most appreciated.

Cordially,

[Director's name]

# *Appendix* B

## ASSESSING ORGANIZATIONAL CLIMATE (AN INFORMAL SURVEY)

Please indicate in the space provided the numeral (0–5) that most accurately describes how you feel about each statement.

| **never** | **seldom** | **sometimes** | **somewhat regularly** | **frequently** | **always** |
|---|---|---|---|---|---|
| 0 | 1 | 2 | 3 | 4 | 5 |

_______ Staff are friendly and trust one another.
_______ Morale is high. There is good team spirit.
_______ Staff are encouraged to learn new skills and competencies.
_______ The center provides guidance for professional advancement.
_______ Supervisor(s) is (are) knowledgeable and competent.
_______ Supervisor(s) provides helpful feedback.
_______ Communication regarding policies and procedures is clear.
_______ Job responsibilities are well defined.
_______ Salaries and fringe benefits are distributed equitably.
_______ Promotions are handled fairly.
_______ Teachers help make decisions about things that directly affect them.
_______ People feel free to express their opinions.
_______ Staff agree on school philosophy and educational objectives.
_______ Staff share a common vision of what the center should be like.
_______ The program is well planned and efficiently run.
_______ Meetings are productive. Time is not wasted.
_______ The work environment is attractive and well organized.
_______ There are sufficient supplies and equipment for staff to do their jobs.
_______ Staff are encouraged to be creative and innovative in their work.
_______ The center implements changes as needed.

What three words describe the climate of this center as a place to work?

What do you perceive to be the greatest strengths of this center?

What areas do you feel could use some improvement?

*Thank you!*

# APPENDIX C

**The Center for Early Childhood Leadership**
6310 Capitol Drive, Wheeling, IL 60090-7201
(800) 443-5522, ext. 7701

## Early Childhood Work Environment Survey

Dear Early Childhood Professional:

This survey is designed to find out how you and your colleagues feel about your early childhood center as a place to work. This questionnaire provides you with an opportunity to express your feelings and opinions concerning various center policies and practices. It includes questions regarding general work conditions, staff relations, supervisor support, pay and promotion opportunities, and the physical setting. The questionnaire should take about 20 minutes to complete. The success of this survey depends on your candid and honest responses. An individual's responses to the survey will not be identified. Results will be reported as group averages that assure anonymity.

When you have completed the survey, put it in the attached plain envelope, seal it, and give it to your staff representative. This individual will then mail the surveys to the Professional Development Project for data analysis. In approximately six to eight weeks your center will receive a center profile. This profile will report a summary of the group results along several dimensions. From this profile, your staff will be able to systematically determine group perceptions of program strengths as well as identify areas that may need improvement.

Thank you for your cooperation and assistance. I hope you find this survey both interesting and useful.

Cordially,

Paula Jorde Bloom

Paula Jorde Bloom, Ph.D.
Project Director

## Background Information

Sex: ☐ Male ☐ Female     Age: _____ Years

What is the highest educational level you have completed?

☐ High School or GED equivalent
☐ Some college
☐ Associate Degree (AA)
☐ Bachelor's Degree (BA/BS)
☐ Some graduate work
☐ Master's Degree (MA/MS)
☐ Post Master's work
☐ Doctorate (Ed.D/Ph.D)

How long have you worked in the field of early childhood? _____ Years _____ Months

How long have you worked for your present employer? _____ Years _____ Months

How long have you worked in your present position? _____ Years _____ Months

Indicate the category that most nearly describes your present employment.

☐ employed full-time (more than 35 hours per week)
☐ employed part-time (20 to 35 hours per week)
☐ employed part-time (10 to 19 hours per week)

How many months of the year are you employed in your position?

☐ year around (12 months)
☐ school year only (9 or 10 months)
☐ fewer than 9 months

Check the job title that most nearly describes your role in your organization. If you have a dual role, what position do you spend ***more*** time doing?

☐ teacher's aide or assistant teacher
☐ classroom teacher or head teacher
☐ assistant director or director
☐ secretary, cook, maintenance
☐ board member
☐ Head Start component coordinator (e.g., education, parent, social service)

# Work Attitudes

Check ***all*** that describe how you feel about your organization:

- ☐ I intend to work here at least two more years
- ☐ I often think of quitting
- ☐ I'm just putting in time
- ☐ I take pride in my center
- ☐ I put a lot of extra effort into my work
- ☐ I feel very committed to this center
- ☐ I don't care what happens to this place after I leave
- ☐ It would be difficult for me to find another job as good as this one
- ☐ It's hard to feel committed to this place
- ☐ I sometimes feel trapped in this job

If you could design the ideal job, how close would your present position resemble this ideal position with respect to the following? *(check 1-5)*

| | *not like my ideal at all* | | *somewhat like my ideal* | | *is my ideal* |
|---|---|---|---|---|---|
| | 1 | 2 | 3 | 4 | 5 |
| relationship with your co-workers | ☐ | ☐ | ☐ | ☐ | ☐ |
| opportunities to learn and grow | ☐ | ☐ | ☐ | ☐ | ☐ |
| relationship with your supervisor | ☐ | ☐ | ☐ | ☐ | ☐ |
| clarity in roles and responsibilities | ☐ | ☐ | ☐ | ☐ | ☐ |
| fairness of pay and promotion opportunities | ☐ | ☐ | ☐ | ☐ | ☐ |
| decision-making structure of the center | ☐ | ☐ | ☐ | ☐ | ☐ |
| agreement among staff on program goals | ☐ | ☐ | ☐ | ☐ | ☐ |
| task orientation, program efficiency | ☐ | ☐ | ☐ | ☐ | ☐ |
| equipment, materials, and the physical setting | ☐ | ☐ | ☐ | ☐ | ☐ |
| innovativeness and creative problem solving | ☐ | ☐ | ☐ | ☐ | ☐ |

Different people want and expect different things from their work. Check the **3** aspects of your work that are most important to you:

- ☐ collegiality, co-worker relations
- ☐ opportunities for professional growth
- ☐ support and feedback from supervisor
- ☐ clarity in policies and procedures
- ☐ fairness in pay, benefits, and promotions
- ☐ involvement in decision making
- ☐ consensus on program goals and objectives
- ☐ accomplishing work in an efficient manner
- ☐ physical setting, sufficient materials
- ☐ innovativeness and creative expression

# Organizational Climate

Please answer the questions in this section with respect to the overall conditions in your center as they are ***most of the time:***

Check ***all*** that describe the staff relations in your center most of the time:

- ☐ cooperative and friendly
- ☐ competitive
- ☐ people are reluctant to express their feelings
- ☐ teachers are very helpful to new staff
- ☐ good team spirit
- ☐ staff are generally frank and candid
- ☐ morale is low
- ☐ people socialize outside of work
- ☐ people feel isolated
- ☐ people complain a lot

Check ***all*** that apply. Does your center...

- ☐ provide on-site staff development workshops?
- ☐ encourage staff to share resources with one another?
- ☐ provide released time to attend conferences?
- ☐ provide released time to visit other schools?
- ☐ provide tuition reimbursement to take college courses?
- ☐ provide guidance for professional advancement?
- ☐ have a library of professional books for staff to use?
- ☐ subscribe to several educational journals and magazines?
- ☐ implement a career ladder for professional advancement?
- ☐ encourage staff to learn new skills and competencies?

Check ***all*** that characterize the supervision provided at your center most of the time:

- ☐ provides support and helpful feedback
- ☐ hard to please
- ☐ unavailable
- ☐ conducts fair evaluations of staff
- ☐ too critical
- ☐ sets high but realistic standards
- ☐ delegates too much
- ☐ compliments and praises staff
- ☐ talks down to staff
- ☐ very knowledgeable

Check ***all*** that apply. Does your program...

- ☐ distribute a parents' handbook detailing policies and procedures?
- ☐ have a staff manual outlining staff policies?
- ☐ provide written contracts for employees?
- ☐ have written job descriptions for each position?
- ☐ distribute a monthly newsletter to parents?

Check ***all*** that characterize your center most of the time:

- ☐ written communication is clear
- ☐ there are seldom conflicting demands made on staff
- ☐ policies and procedures are well-defined
- ☐ rules are consistent
- ☐ staff are well-informed

Check ***all*** that describe the pay and promotion system at your center:

- ☐ salaries are fair considering the center's income
- ☐ promotions are not handled fairly
- ☐ pay and benefits are equitably distributed
- ☐ some people are paid more than they are worth
- ☐ raises are based on favoritism
- ☐ steps are being taken to increase pay and benefits
- ☐ pay is fair compared to what other centers pay
- ☐ this place is a revolving door, no job security
- ☐ people are taken advantage of
- ☐ chances for promotion are good

Check ***all*** that describe how decisions are made at your center most of the time:

- ☐ people are encouraged to be self-sufficient in making decisions
- ☐ the director likes to make most of the decisions
- ☐ people don't feel free to express their opinions
- ☐ everyone provides input on the content of staff meetings
- ☐ conformity is the name of the game here
- ☐ there are scheduled staff meetings at least twice a month
- ☐ people provide input but decisions have already been made
- ☐ teachers make decisions about things that directly affect them
- ☐ teachers are seldom asked their opinion on issues
- ☐ the director values everyone's input for major decisions

Listed below are some common organizational decisions and actions. How much influence does the teaching staff ***currently have*** in each of the areas below:

| | *very little influence* | *some influence* | *considerable influence* |
|---|---|---|---|
| Ordering materials/supplies | ☐ | ☐ | ☐ |
| Interviewing/hiring new staff | ☐ | ☐ | ☐ |
| Determining program objectives | ☐ | ☐ | ☐ |
| Training new aides/teachers | ☐ | ☐ | ☐ |
| Planning daily schedule of activities | ☐ | ☐ | ☐ |

How much influence do you think the teaching staff ***would like to have*** in each of these areas:

| | *very little influence* | *some influence* | *considerable influence* |
|---|---|---|---|
| Ordering materials/supplies | ☐ | ☐ | ☐ |
| Interviewing/hiring new staff | ☐ | ☐ | ☐ |
| Determining program objectives | ☐ | ☐ | ☐ |
| Training new aides/teachers | ☐ | ☐ | ☐ |
| Planning daily schedule of activities | ☐ | ☐ | ☐ |

Check ***all*** that apply with respect to the goals of your program:

- ☐ goals are left vague
- ☐ everyone agrees on program goals
- ☐ people know how to compromise
- ☐ center does not have a written philosophy
- ☐ staff share a common vision of what the center should be like
- ☐ the staff seldom talk about educational objectives
- ☐ staff are committed to program goals
- ☐ staff are not unified in their philosophy
- ☐ people disagree on what should be taught to children
- ☐ program has well-defined educational objectives

Check ***all*** that describe the way things get done at your center most of the time:

- ☐ meetings are a waste of time
- ☐ this place is run very efficiently
- ☐ people get the job done
- ☐ time is wasted
- ☐ deadlines are missed regularly
- ☐ things rarely get put off
- ☐ employees work hard
- ☐ people come to work late
- ☐ people procrastinate often
- ☐ meetings are productive

Check ***all*** that apply to the physical environment of your center:

- ☐ efficient use of space
- ☐ cramped and crowded conditions
- ☐ seems either too hot or too cold
- ☐ neat, tidy, and safe
- ☐ decorations are drab
- ☐ teachers have a place to store personal belongings
- ☐ classroom noise disrupts office business
- ☐ there are sufficient supplies and materials
- ☐ the building needs major repairs
- ☐ storage space is well-organized

Check ***all*** that describe your program as a whole:

- ☐ emphasizes creativity
- ☐ not very innovative
- ☐ quite traditional
- ☐ implements needed changes
- ☐ encourages diverse opinions
- ☐ regularly looks at new educational approaches
- ☐ things stay pretty much the same
- ☐ new ideas are tried out
- ☐ people avoid taking risks at all costs
- ☐ problems are not addressed

Rank order the following program objectives according to their importance at your center during the next year. Put a *1* by the most important, a *2* by the next most important and so on until you get to *6* for the least important. Each objective must have only ***one*** number next to it.

*In our program, it is important...*

_____ to help children develop language and problem-solving skills

_____ to help children build strong friendships and learn to share

_____ to help children master concepts needed for reading and arithmetic

_____ to help children develop skill and independence in caring for themselves

_____ to help children develop physical coordination

_____ to help children develop a healthy self-esteem and positive self-concept

How long did it take you to complete this survey? ______ minutes

We appreciate your cooperation in taking the time to answer the questions in this survey. If you have any additional comments you would like to add, feel free to do so in the space below. Again, thank you.

# APPENDIX D

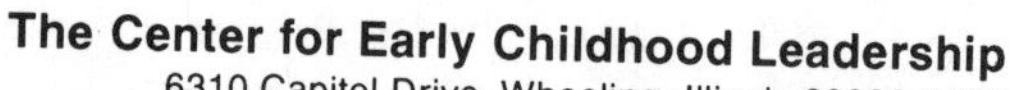

**The Center for Early Childhood Leadership**
6310 Capitol Drive, Wheeling, Illinois 60090-7201
(800) 443-5522, ext. 7701

## WORK ENVIRONMENT PROFILE

**Name:** THE CHILDREN'S PLACE

**Date:** October 23, 1994

**Total administrative, teaching, and support staff:** 15

**Code:** 0000

**Number of staff completing survey:** 15

**Employment pattern of respondents:**

8 **employed full-time (35 hours per week or more)**
5 **employed part-time (20-34 hours per week)**
2 **employed part-time (10-19 hours per week)**
0 **data not provided by respondent**

**PART A. ORGANIZATIONAL CLIMATE (N = 15 )**

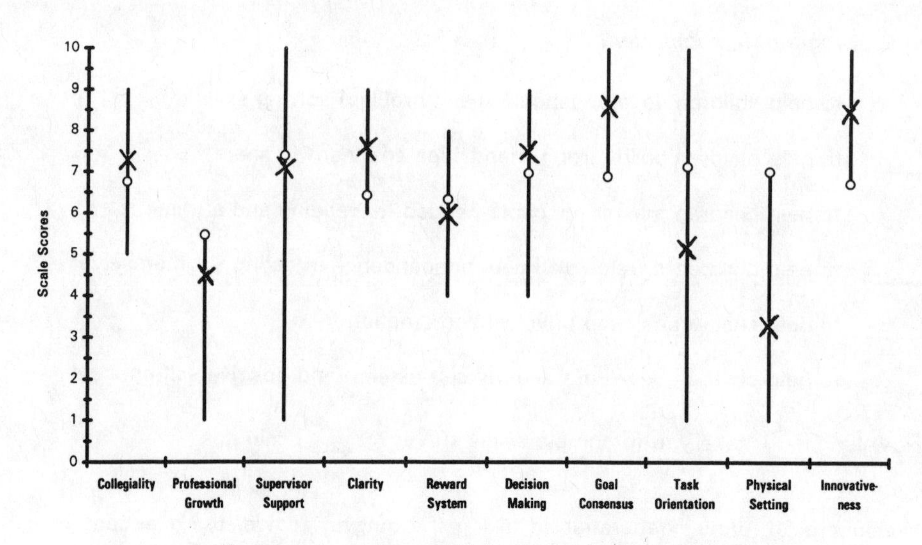


**The X represents the average score for this dimension for subjects included in this sample.**
**The O represents the norm for this dimension based on responses of 5,251 workers in 421 centers.**
**The vertical line for each dimension represents the range of scores for subjects in this sample.**

**PART B. SUMMARY OF WORKER VALUES (N = 15 )**

Number of employees who indicated each dimension as being one of three most important to them.

| | | | |
|---|---|---|---|
| 3 | Collegiality, co-worker relations | 5 | Involvement in decision making |
| 10 | Opportunities for professional growth | 2 | Consensus on program goals, objectives |
| 4 | Support and feedback from supervisor | 2 | Accomplishing work in efficient manner |
| 3 | Clarity in policies and procedures | 9 | Physical setting, sufficient materials |
| 5 | Equitable pay, benefits, and promotions | 2 | Innovativeness and creative expression |

**PART C. SUMMARY OF OVERALL COMMITMENT TO THE ORGANIZATION (N = 15 )**

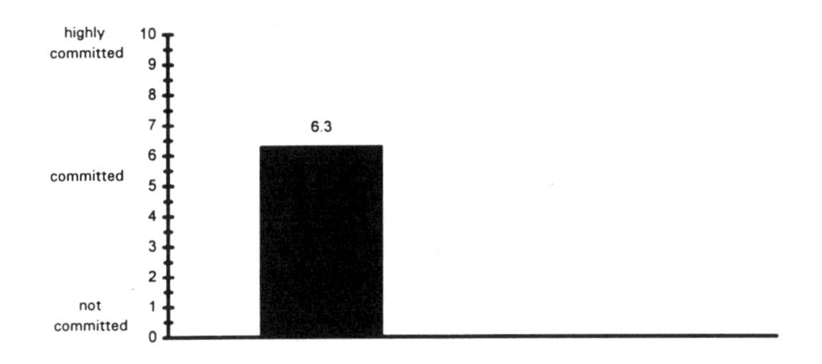


**PART D. SUMMARY OF HOW CURRENT WORK ENVIRONMENT RESEMBLES IDEAL (N = 14 )**

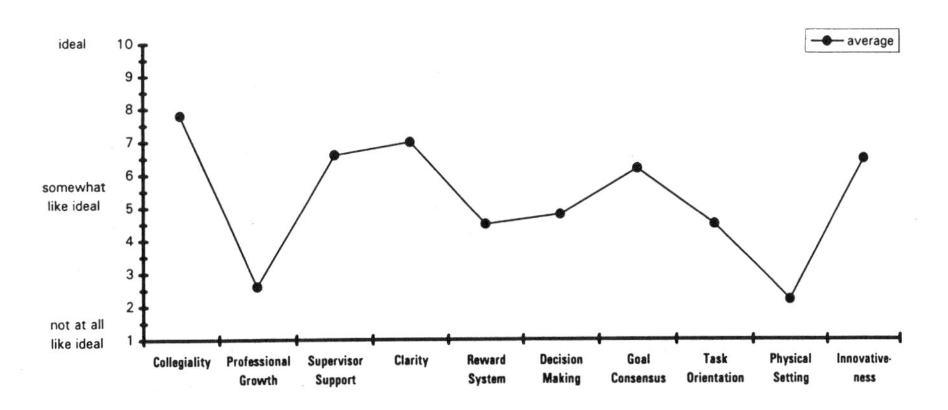

**PART E. RANKING OF VARIOUS EDUCATIONAL GOALS AND OBJECTIVES (N = 14 )**

| | Number of subjects who ranked item as | | | | | |
|---|---|---|---|---|---|---|
| To help children develop... | 1 | 2 | 3 | 4 | 5 | 6 |
| *language and problem solving skills* | 0 | 1 | 2 | 6 | 5 | 0 |
| *strong friendships, skills in sharing* | 3 | 0 | 4 | 3 | 2 | 2 |
| *concepts needed for reading and math* | 0 | 1 | 0 | 1 | 2 | 10 |
| *independence in caring for themselves* | 0 | 10 | 3 | 0 | 1 | 0 |
| *physical skill and coordination* | 0 | 1 | 3 | 4 | 4 | 2 |
| *positive self-concepts and self-esteem* | 11 | 1 | 2 | 0 | 0 | 0 |

**PART F. DEGREE OF INFLUENCE OF THE TEACHING STAFF REGARDING VARIOUS ORGANIZATIONAL DECISIONS (N = 15 )**

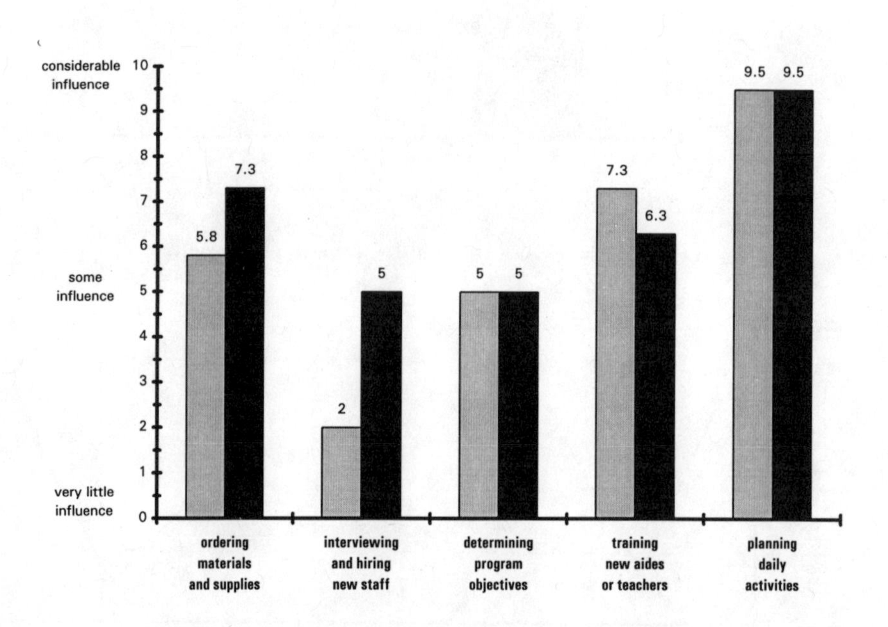

# *INDEX*

## BY SUBJECT

## BY AUTHOR

# *Information about NAEYC*

***NAEYC is . . .***

an organization of nearly 102,000 members, founded in 1926, that is committed to fostering the growth and development of children from birth through age 8. Membership is open to all who share a desire to serve young children and act on behalf of the needs and rights of all children.

***NAEYC provides . . .***

educational services and resources to adults and programs working with and for children, including

• ***Young Children,*** *the* peer-reviewed journal for early childhood educators

• **Books, posters, brochures, position statements, and videos** to expand your knowledge and commitment and support your work with young children and families, including such topics as inclusion, diversity, literacy, guidance, assessment, developmentally appropriate practice, and teaching

• **An Annual Conference,** the largest education conference in North America, that brings people together from across the United States and other countries to share their expertise and advocate on behalf of children and families

• **Week of the Young Child** celebrations planned annually by NAEYC Affiliate Groups in communities around the country to call public attention to the critical significance of the child's early years

• **Insurance plans** for members and programs

• **Public affairs information,** and access to information through NAEYC resources and communication systems, for conducting knowledgeable advocacy efforts at all levels of government and in the media

• **A voluntary accreditation system** for high-quality programs for children through the National Academy of Early Childhood Programs

• **Professional development resources and programs** through the National Institute for Early Childhood Professional Development, working to improve the quality and consistency of early childhood preparation and leadership opportunities

• **Young Children International** to promote international communication, discussion forums, and information exchanges

For information about membership, publications, or other NAEYC services, visit NAEYC online at **www.naeyc.org**

**National Association for the Education of Young Children**
**1509 16th Street, NW, Washington, DC 20036-1426**
**202-232-8777 or 800-424-2460**